VILLAGE
LIVERPOOL

© The Bluecoat Press 2009

Published by The Bluecoat Press, Liverpool
Book design by Michael March, Liverpool
Printed by Tenon and Polert Colour Scanning Ltd.

ISBN 9781904438878

Acknowledgements
I would like to thank Ruth Hobbins and David Stoker, of Liverpool Record Office, for
permission to reproduce the pictures in this book, Keith Jones, the grandson of
A.H. Jones, for additional information about his grandfather, and my husband, who
accompanied me to some of the further flung corners of Liverpool.

VILLAGE LIVERPOOL

Kay Parrott

The Bluecoat Press

CONTENTS

Map of Lancashire, 1837, Thomas Moule. The town of Liverpool had not embraced Everton at this time, which is shown as a separate village.

INTRODUCTION

This book depicts the suburbs of Liverpool as shown mainly in the watercolours of two artists, Frederick Beattie, who was working at the beginning of the twentieth century and Alfred Harry Jones, painting just after World War II and in the early 1950s. There are also a few pictures by the nineteenth century artists W.G. and William Herdman, and Allan P. Tankard, who, like A.H. Jones, was working in Liverpool in the 1940s and 1950s. All these paintings are in the Watercolours Collection, in Liverpool Record Office, Central Library, William Brown Street and I am grateful to David Stoker, manager of the Record Office for allowing me to reproduce them here. Other books have been published, which show the city centre, here we look at what, in many cases, was still a rural landscape of sandstone cottages set in farmland, with a number of small villages or rural centres. Every effort has been made to show as wide a range of pictures of Liverpool's suburbs as possible, but it was the artists who made the initial selection of scenes they were to paint. What we may now consider to be local landmarks have often not been painted and the selection has been made from the available views. Often the artists would visit an area and paint a series of scenes, for example, there are nearly twenty views of Hale by Jones in the Liverpool Record Office collection; sometimes it is almost possible to follow the artist's route as he moved around. For the purposes of this book the city has been divided into ten separate areas, although in some cases, such as Old Swan, Broadgreen and Childwall, several suburbs have been combined in one area. There is a small selection of pictures of Hale and Huyton, just beyond the city's boundaries.

LIVERPOOL

Liverpool has grown from a small fishing village on the banks of the River Mersey to the large conurbation of today. The city's growth can be likened to the layers of half an onion, each new period of growth forming an extra layer around the old core as it has spread outwards. The original settlement, dating from the grant of letters patent by King John in 1207, consisted of just seven streets: Dale Street, Water Street, Chapel Street and More (now Tithebarn) Street ran down to the river, with Mill (or Milne, now Old Hall Street) Street, Juggler Street and Castle Street at right angles and parallel to the Mersey. By the time that John Chadwick produced the first surveyed map of the town in 1725 it had extended little beyond these streets and there was still open countryside the far end of Dale Street.

The early years of the nineteenth century saw a gradual growth beyond these boundaries. The dock system expanded to the north and housing, generally of poor quality, followed the docks to provide a ready source of cheap, casual labour, in the Vauxhall area. Wealthy merchants moved out from the congested, polluted and noisy town centre to the airy heights of Everton and to elegant houses around Abercromby Square, Canning Street and Rodney Street. This process continued and they moved further into what was then the country; as transport improved they were able to travel to work in the centre of Liverpool yet live in comfort in their newly built semi-rural villas. As they moved outwards the expanding population spread behind them. Respectable working-class terraced housing was constructed in Toxteth Park, Anfield and Kensington, but the overcrowded court and slum dwellings still remained.

In the twentieth century the physical area occupied by the city grew enormously as the population reached a peak of nearly 800,000 in 1951. Liverpool was a pioneer in social housing and as a result of slum clearance starting in the 1930s large council estates were built on what were then the outskirts, in places such as Norris Green and Speke. In contrast there was also a growth in private housing of the type associated with suburbia, and large areas, such as Mossley Hill, Childwall and West Derby, were covered with estates of semi-detached, privately owned, homes. An acute housing shortage after World War II led to the construction of more council estates in the 1950s and 60s, including this time high-rise blocks, seen then as the solution to the city's housing problems. Large council estates were built at Childwall Valley and Croxteth, and also beyond the city boundaries at Kirkby and Skelmersdale. A decade later housing development had reached six miles from the city centre with the building of the Netherley estate.

THE ARTISTS

Frederick Beattie, born February 1851 in Liverpool, and his brother Edwin Robert, also an artist, were the sons of Robert Beattie, a well known Liverpool portrait painter. However due to Frederick's poor health the family moved to Southport shortly after he was born. After studying architecture in Liverpool, he, and another, younger brother, went to Grand Haven on the eastern shore of Lake Michigan in the United States, with the intention of working in the timber trade, but actually ended up working in a lumber camp. They lived in a shanty, built and furnished themselves using plunder from a wreck which came ashore near their cabin and supporting themselves by the sale of Frederick's paintings. They decided to return to England via Canada and journeyed, on foot, to

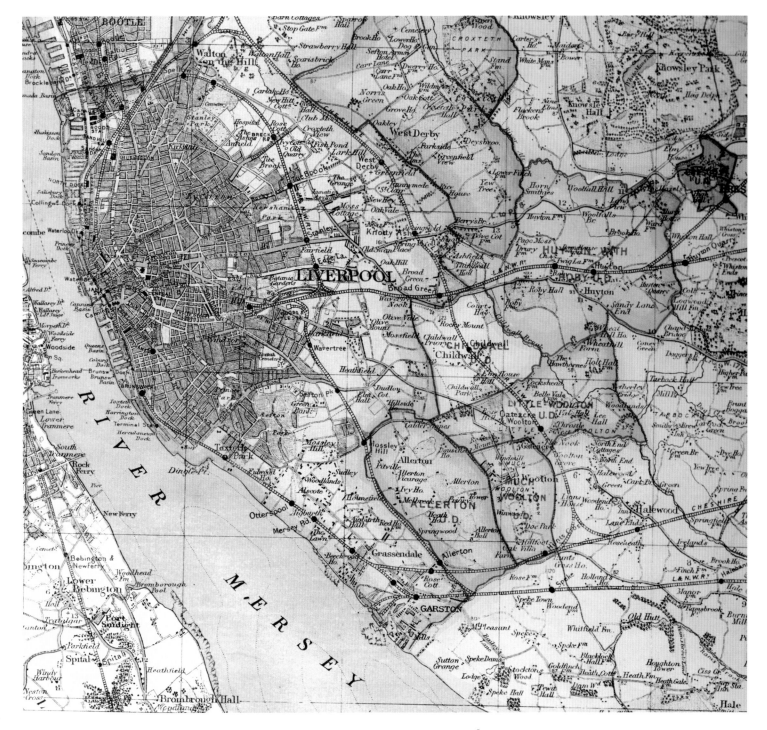

Bacon's Map of Lancashire, 1903. Liverpool had absorbed Everton, Walton, Wavertree and Garston, athough Allerton, Childwall, West Derby and Woolton remained as separate urban district councils.

Ordnance Survey, 1937. A century after the Thomas Moule map, and the village character of the area had virtually disappeared.

Montreal, then worked their passage back to Liverpool. Frederick appears to have been restless and fond of the vagabond way of life, often going on extended camping and painting trips to north Wales or Scotland with his brother Edwin. He died in Liverpool in July 1913 and is buried in the churchyard of St. Anne, Stanley. The works of both Frederick and Edwin are represented in the Beattie Collection in Liverpool Record Office, but Frederick is the only brother who seems to have painted in the suburbs and it is his work which is included in this book.

Alfred Harry Jones was born in Liverpool in 1891 and was awarded several school prizes for art. However he was not a professional artist and was self-taught. Gassed in the trenches of the Great War, he learnt to appreciate the tranquillity and comfort of quiet rural and urban places, often reflected in his work, where there are few people and the emphasis is on the view. He worked, somewhat prosaically, as a canned goods broker, at 42 Stanley Street in the centre of the city and lived in Moorcroft Road, Allerton. In 1947 an exhibition of his watercolours was held at the Hugo Lang Gallery in Whitechapel, with views which included Kirkby Lonsdale, north Wales and Egypt, as well as Liverpool. J.F.S. (probably J.F. Smith, the City Librarian) writing in the introduction to the catalogue of the exhibition remarks that

'Mr Jones has taken up the brush and palette laid down by Herdman and is, in the same way, preserving memories of the city's landmarks and quiet places for the historical interest of future generations'. The reference to W.G. Herdman is significant, as he and his son, William, had similarly painted topographical views of Liverpool a century earlier. A.H. Jones died in 1958 aged just 67, succumbing to the loss of one lung so many years earlier. He had lost one son at 7 years of age to Scarlet fever, which had also had a profound effect on him. His widow, Audrey, however, survived him for many years to just short of her 100th birthday. He was also survived by his other son and grandson.

The author of an article in the Liverpool Echo in 1930, regretted the change in character of 'our suburbs' brought about by new roads and the spread of housing, and remembered 'the countrified aspect' and quiet roads down which it was 'a soothing pleasure on a summer's evening, to wind along between their mossy, red sandstone walls, with the line of grand old trees arching overhead; past grassy demesne and wooded estate; past snug cottage house, dairy and poultry farm, into country innocent ... of rushing traffic ...' It is this sometimes forgotten aspect of Liverpool's history which is depicted in this book.

WEST DERBY AND BEYOND

The village of West Derby is mentioned in the Domesday Book and was probably the most important of the Hundreds into which the county of Lancashire was divided, if only because it is mentioned first and has the longest entry. At that time it was more important than Liverpool, then only a small fishing settlement on the banks of the Mersey. However by the early thirteenth century West Derby had declined in relative importance as Liverpool started to grow. A motte and bailey castle, built by the Normans but having its origins in Saxon times, stood on a site to the north of St. Mary's Church for about two hundred years. From the Middle Ages West Derby was an important legal centre being the site of the local manor court and the court house in the centre of the village was still used as late as the early twentieth century, although just once a year, to settle local land disputes. The first reference to a chapel in the village occurs in the fourteenth century when there was a chapel of ease, created for the inhabitants of the outlying parish,

for St. Mary's Church, Walton on the Hill, but the area did not acquire parish status and its own church, St. Mary's, until 1844. In the early nineteenth century the village was still a quiet agricultural district, but its population expanded during the century to over 100,000. Sixty large houses were built during this time for the merchants and shipowners of the rapidly growing city of Liverpool. It was described as "a quiet and secluded place of residence suitable for people of refinement and taste". These mansions all required servants and the housing for them contributed further to the village's expansion. Horse buses, and later horse drawn trams, ran from the centre of Liverpool to West Derby village for the convenience of local businessmen. In 1896 the first telephones were installed in the area, although electricity did not arrive until 1927. The southern area of West Derby became part of the city of Liverpool in 1895, but the area to the north-east remained a separate township until 1928.

ALFRED. H. JONES.

Yeoman's House, West Derby village, 1951.
A.H. Jones, A.H. Jones Collection 161.

Built in 1660, or according to some sources 1586, this is usually referred to as the 'Yeoman's House', being an example of the sort of house which a yeoman of that time could afford to build. The small stone mullioned windows are typical of the period and although built of sandstone it has been whitewashed for many years. It is now officially number 10 Almond's Green, but numbered 10 West Derby Village when this picture was painted. In the first decades of the twentieth century it was occupied by R. Wearing and Sons, builders, and by 1949 was home to the Misses Rachel and Mary Jane Fitton, as well as, somewhat oddly, the Liverpool Street Scaffolding Company. The garage of John Gibson, motor engineer, to the left, was once the premises of Hooper and Simmons, coachbuilders, established in about 1879.

F. BEATTIE. 1910

There are records of a school in West Derby as early as 1667 and in 1825 a new school was built, near the Chapel, which had space for 60 pupils, using money raised by public subscription. Presumably as the local population grew this building was no longer adequate and in 1859 the Earl of Sefton gave land for a new school in Meadow Lane, seen in this picture. It was built at a cost of £4,985, with the money once again raised by public subscription, and administered by St. Mary's Parish Church in the village. Originally intended for the poorer children of the neighbourhood, it later became West Derby National School. This building in turn was replaced by a new school in 1974, although parts of the 1860s school have been incorporated into the new structure.

Deysbrook Farm, Deysbrook Lane, West Derby, 1951.
A.H. Jones, A.H. Jones Collection 160.

Even in 1951 there was still farmland close to the centre of West Derby village and Deysbrook Farm was situated at the junction of Deysbrook Lane and Beavan's Lane. This view shows the old brick barn, with its large open arches which would allow the hay to dry. In front is a conveyor belt, probably used to move the hay into the barn. Jones calls this England's Farm, possibly a reference to a previous tenant, although in 1949 it was occupied by James Oliver Gaskell. Today the site is covered with houses.

Deysbrook Lane, West Derby, 1951.
A.H. Jones, A.H. Jones Collection 159.

This view shows numbers 20 to 46, Deysbrook Lane, situated between Lisleholme Close and, in the distance, Mercer Place. These houses formed part of a row of similar terraced houses about 250 yards long, with the Derby Arms public house on the corner of Mercer Place. Today these houses have been replaced by semis. The trees on the right fringe the Francis Xavier College recreation ground, which in the 1950s became Melwood, Liverpool Football Club's training ground. The priests who taught the boys football were Fathers Melling and Woodcock, hence the name Melwood.

Deysbrook Lane, West Derby, 1951.
A.H. Jones, A.H. Jones Collection 158.

This is a close-up of number 30 Deysbrook Lane, part of the terrace shown in the previous view. A porch has been added to the property and the small front garden replaced by cobbles, which makes it stand out from the others in the row. In 1949 it was occupied by Miss Jessie Moss and at this date women were the head of the household of many of these cottages, perhaps reflecting their modest size

The Dog and Gun Inn stood at the crossroads of Carr Lane East, Stonebridge Lane and Croxteth Hall Lane. The building, shown here, was constructed in the 1930s, greatly extending an earlier one. In 1927 the proprietor was Philip Maher and at that date the facilities offered included 'good accommodation for cyclists and travellers, good stabling', as well as a bowling green. By 1949, when this picture was painted, the licensee was Denis Ryan. The inn gave its name to a school, established some time before 1875, and a post office, as well as the surrounding hamlet. After World War II an extensive estate of Corporation houses was built in the Croxteth area. The public house closed in 2004 after problems with drug dealers and has subsequently been demolished, although the area is still known by this name.

This view, also at the junction of Carr Lane East and Croxteth Hall Lane, looks in the opposite direction to the previous painting, with the Dog and Gun Inn to our right, out of view. Immediately opposite is the local police station, surprisingly large for what would have been a

Carr Lane East, 1950.
A.H. Jones, A.H. Jones Collection 138.

relatively rural community when it was built; on the opposite corner stood a branch of the Liverpool Co-operative Society. The police station was demolished in the 1950s, when large numbers of council houses were built in the area. The lorry and van, shown here, contrast with the horses and carts shown in a number of the paintings by F. Beattie forty years earlier, at the beginning of the twentieth century.

This house stood on Lower House Lane, between West Derby Cemetery and Carr Lane East, approximately where Storrington Avenue is today. From its style it was probably built in the early nineteenth century. In 1949 it was occupied by Arthur Gordon, a labourer, but, judging by the state of the garden, appears by this date to be somewhat neglected. Note the detail, added by the artist, of a black cat sitting on the left downstairs window ledge.

Longmoor Grove is a short road, situated off Longmoor Lane, opposite what is now Inglis Road, and when this picture was painted it consisted of just three pairs of semi-detached cottages. This view shows numbers 7 to 11, occupied in 1949 by a railway porter, a manager and someone without an occupation. Sandy Lane, leading to Higher Lane, is at the end of the road. Today the houses have been demolished and the land they occupied is a small area of open ground.

Longmoor Lane, 1950.
A.H. Jones, A.H. Jones Collection 150.

This group of cottages, numbers 193 to 197 Longmoor Lane, was situated opposite Longmoor Grove, between Inglis Road and a road intriguingly named 'Ancient Meadows'. Judging by the position of the chimneys and front doors, the two cottages on the left are smaller and were probably built at a different date to that on the right. The low grey building to their right is the premises of William Wren and Sons, building contractors. Today the street name has been retained but new houses have been built there.

TUEBROOK AND WALTON

The suburb of Tuebrook takes its name from the Tew or Tue Brook, a 'mysterious stream' which '…rolled pleasantly through… the outer fields' from its source into the River Alt at Fazakerley. The area centres on the junction of Green Lane and West Derby Road, where the striking church of St. John the Baptist stands, with nineteenth century terraced housing to the west and 1930s Corporation estates to the east. The village of Walton, around the parish church of St. Mary, dates back to Anglo-Saxon times, is mentioned in the Domesday Book, and was for many years a more important settlement than Liverpool. The church served all the surrounding area and Liverpool did not become a separate parish until 1699, Walton itself was incorporated into the city only in 1895. In the early twentieth century much of the area was still largely agricultural, with isolated farms. Encroaching urbanisation was typified by the construction of Queens Drive, Liverpool's ring road, designed by City Engineer, James Brodie. By 1912 six miles of this road had been constructed through what was then, in most cases, open country, the earliest building work taking place in Walton.

Girvan House, 1906.
F. Beattie, Beattie Collection 306.

Girvan House, number 505, West Derby Road, stood with several other detached houses, between Victoria Road and Lisburn Lane. In 1901 it was home to William Craze, a fruit merchant. After the house was demolished, it became the site of a branch of the Bank of Liverpool, built about 1910 at the renumbered 611 West Derby Road by Francis Doyle, with Charles F. Frater as the first manager. This later became Martin's, then Barclay's Bank and today it is a delicatessen.

Tue Brook House, West Derby Road, 1910.
F. Beattie, Beattie Collection 25.

This old sandstone house, limewashed for many years, with a stone flagged roof, still survives, although it now stands beside the busy dual carriageway at Mill Bank. Liverpool's oldest dated house, it is thought to have been built in 1615 for John Mercer, a yeoman farmer, and

Beattie reproduces, at the top right, the datestone from the building. In 1921 it was taken over by the Corporation as part of the Larkhill estate and rented as a council house. It

is said to have a priest's hole and a 'shy ghost'. In 1896 it was described as 'original and unrestored ... the only addition ... a lean-to scullery at the back of the kitchen' and for many years was occupied by a Mr Fletcher, who carried out his business as a wheelwright there.

These old cottages still stand on the south side of West Derby Road, nearly opposite Tue Brook House; the junction of Gardner Road can just be seen to the right. The house on the right, number 354, is probably as old, or may be even older than, Tue Brook House, but has been

much altered. What was once a single-storey stone built, thatched cottage, has had a floor added and the thatch replaced by slate. To the left, number 358, has the appearance of a later stuccoed Georgian house, with an arched doorway and traceried fanlight, but may be equally ancient. In 1909 number 354 was home to John Bolton, a labourer, and William Knight, a general contractor, lived at number 358.

F. BEATTIE 1910

This imposing house, Barnfield, stood at the junction of what were then Larkhill and Mill Lanes. The local tithebarn once stood here and it is now the site of the Jolly Miller public house. Thomas Toulmin, an attorney, built the house in about 1828 and lived there for many years, although by 1870 Charles E. Dixon, a steamship owner and merchant, was resident there. In the 1930s the house was demolished to make way for the Jolly Miller, which took its name from the old West Derby Mill which stood opposite and in turn gave its name to Mill Lane.

FRED BEATTIE, 1909

Junction of Derby Lane and Black Horse Lane, 1909.
F. Beattie, Beattie Collection 301.

This rural scene, looking eastwards along Black Horse Lane, shows the area when there were still open fields, although it was sufficiently urban even then to have had street lights, and the tide of terrace housing was gradually spreading eastwards from Old Swan.

Behind the viewer stood Moss House, built by Peter Rigby, a Liverpool merchant and mayor of the town in 1774. When the Stoneycroft section of Queens Drive was built in about 1912, it partly followed the route of Black Horse Lane, with only the southern 400 yards of the road remaining, and the junction shown here became a busy intersection.

This picture shows the source of the Tue (or Tew) Brook, from which the suburb takes its name. Beattie identifies this as being in what is now Lister Drive, although others have suggested that it was further east. Yates and Perry's map of 1768 shows the brook flowing westwards, parallel with Green Lane, crossing West Derby Road (then called Tew-brook Lane), before it eventually joined the River Alt at Fazakerley. Green Lane was once a little frequented shortcut between West Derby Road and Prescot Road, just a narrow pathway between bracken, gorse and wild hyacinths. Today the brook has been culverted and, flowing underground, has been all but forgotten. Lister Drive is the site of a large power station, built in 1902, public baths (now closed and currently used as a pet shop), a school (demolished in 2005) and a library (also closed); Green Lane itself has long since been built up.

St. Mary's Church, Walton on the Hill, 1820.
W.G. Herdman, Herdman Collection 1472.

Unlike Liverpool, which at the time was just a small fishing village on the banks of the River Mersey, Walton on the Hill is recorded in the Domesday Book and its church, St. Mary, served as parish church for the whole area until Liverpool was acquired its own parish and church in 1699. Although there has been a church on the site for centuries, it has been much altered. In 1743 the nave was rebuilt and the chancel in 1810. This view painted in 1820 depicts the north side of the church, before the tower was reconstructed in 1828-31. Unfortunately the building was severely damaged by air raids in May 1941 and, although the 1820s tower remained, the rest of the building had to be reconstructed once again.

The Guide's House, Walton, undated.
W.G. Herdman, Herdman Collection 1468.

Until the middle of the nineteenth century this ancient house stood in Walton village on the main road from Liverpool to Ormskirk. From here travellers, either in coaches or on foot, could hire a guide to assist them on the difficult road ahead and protect them from footpads who lay in wait for the unwary.

Church Lane, Walton, 1946.
A.H. Jones, A.H. Jones Collection 35.

This view of Church Lane looks from its junction with Smithy Lane, towards Rice Lane. On the left-hand side is the wall of St. Mary's Church, Walton, the former parish church of Liverpool. Ye Olde Beehive is believed to have been the oldest licensed house in Liverpool. The public house on the corner of Rice Lane, in the distance on the right, was Ye Olde Brown Cow. In 1911 Samuel Clarkson was carrying out his trade as blacksmith at number 5 and thirty five years later, in 1946, the date of this picture, he was at the same address, still plying the same trade.

32

New Hall Farm, 1912.
F. Beattie, Beattie Collection 21.

New Hall, which was situated at the junction of New Hall Lane and Broad Lane, became the property of the Molyneux family in the late sixteenth century, and their main residence in the eighteenth century. The house itself had a datestone for 1660. In the nineteenth century the Liverpool banker Arthur Heywood acquired the estate and in 1926 the house was demolished. This view shows the farm associated with the Hall, which in 1911 was occupied by William Jackson. The Cheshire Lines railway, linking Southport in the north with the Liverpool and Manchester Railway to the south, was built close by.

Townsend Lane, 1909.
F. Beattie, Beattie Collection 316.

This is Rose Cottage, situated on the north side of Townsend Lane, close to its junction with Maiden Lane, and was obviously a farm house, with the barn and house joined together. The scene looks very rural, with fields just beyond the buildings, but new terrace housing was gradually spreading eastwards as roads were built on either side of Townsend Lane. However, perhaps surprisingly, the tide of new houses did not reach this spot and the open space on either side of the road remains as playing fields or recreation ground. Just to the left of the house Townsend Lane ran beneath the London and North Western Railway, linking Edge Hill and Bootle, with Breck Road Station just north of the bridge.

THE INNER SUBURBS:
EVERTON, KIRKDALE AND EDGE HILL

Everton is situated on a sandstone ridge to the north of central Liverpool, rising to a height of 250, this was once an area of common land, with heath, furze bushes and poor pasture. Until the end of the eighteenth century Everton "slumbered on as a quiet and retired agricultural hamlet". However the early nineteenth century was a time of change as wealthy Liverpool merchants moved out of the noisy, congested, dirty town centre to the higher ground, open space and cleaner air of Everton, where they built substantial houses. As the city expanded outwards in the mid-nineteenth century the tide of small terraced houses reached Everton, the merchants moved further out to places like Allerton and West Derby and by the end of the century the area was entirely built up. In the 1960s much of this terraced housing was demolished, to be replaced by high rise tower blocks. These proved to be deeply unpopular and lasted for a much shorter time than the old terraced houses. Today houses have once again been built here, but to a much lower density than formerly, and there are once again large areas of open space, with views to the River Mersey and the Welsh hills beyond.

In the nineteenth century Kirkdale, between the ridge of Everton and the River Mersey, was once an area of densely packed houses intermingled with industries such as tanning, glass making, brewing, soap, alkali and vitriol manufacture, turpentine distilling and iron foundries. But like Everton, until the end of the eighteenth century, the area had been overwhelmingly rural and formed an "agreeable country retreat, away from the smoke and noise of the bustling town, with green fields on either side." Much of the industry and houses have now gone, the slums were replaced by tenements in the 1930s and most of these have also been cleared, although regeneration of the area continues with projects such as the Eldonian Village. Edge Hill, to the east of the city centre, is situated on a continuation of the same ridge as Everton and has had a similar history. Better quality housing was built here in the early nineteenth century, although more of this survives than in Everton. However the area was similarly engulfed by terraced housing later in the century, which was replaced by 1930s tenements and now by low density housing.

Barlow Lane, Kirkdale, c.1866.
W.G. Herdman, Herdman Collection 299A.

Barlow Lane is a short stretch of road linking Westminster Road to the junction of Walton Road and County Road and this view shows a number of old cottages on the north side of the road, close to its junction with Westminster Road. In the mid 1860s the cottages were occupied by, amongst others, a gardener, a market gardener, a cowkeeper, two book keepers and a shipwright.

The picturesque cottages in this road obviously had an attraction for local artists and Frederick Beattie painted here fifty years after W.G. Herdman. The properties pre-date much of the terraced housing

Barlow Lane, Kirkdale, 1909.
F. Beattie, Beattie Collection 17.

built in the area in the late nineteenth century, which certainly would not have had the gardens

depicted here. In 1907 the Misses Elizabeth and Margaret Wood, who lived at number 15, were described as 'cowkeepers' and they doubtless sold milk from the dairy shown here.

Fordham Street was a short road off Walton Road, not far from Barlow Lane, opposite Springfield Square. This picture shows the rear of houses at the far end of the road. The building on the left is the back of the public house at 62-4 Barlow Street run in 1911 by Walter James and the passageway leads through to the adjoining Barlow Street. Just to the right of this view was the rear of St. Lawrence's Church of England Primary School.

This mill, built in the early nineteenth century and shown on James Sherriff's Map of the environs of Liverpool, published in 1823, was situated in Springfield Square, just off Walton Road and close to Barlow Lane. When Beattie painted this view in the early years of the twentieth century the mill was unused and had lost its sails. Today the square still exists, but the mill has been replaced by light industrial units, although the Springfield Hotel, on the corner of Walton Road, remains.

Walton Breck Road, 1911.
F. Beattie, Beattie Collection 96.

This solid looking building, unusually for a building of this size in Liverpool, was built of stone rather than brick, and stood on the southern side of Walton Breck Road, near its junction with Breck Road, at the rear of the Cabbage Hall Inn. They were known as Broadbent's Cottages, from the 1830s proprietor of the inn, John Broadbent. Although it appears to be one dwelling it actually consisted of a cluster of four separate houses; two entrances can just be seen in the left-hand gable end and there would have been another two on the opposite end. According to the 1911 street directory of Liverpool they were occupied by a contractor, a fitter and two ladies, Mrs Jane Houldsworth and Mrs Elizabeth Hickey, neither of whom gave an occupation.

St. Domingo Road, Everton, 1911.
F. Beattie, Beattie Collection 16.

This house stood at the corner of St. Domingo Road and Mark Street and the name, Mark's Rock, which the artist has enlarged, was obviously engraved over the gateway leading to the garden on St. Domingo Road. This area had once been part of the local common land and was gradually built up in the early nineteenth century. Before the houses were built there had been an extensive view from this spot, westward over the River Mersey, to North Wales and even the Derbyshire hills. In the east Prescot, Knowsley Park and Hall, Croxteth Park and Hall, Garswood, Billinge Beacon and Ashurst Beacon could all be seen. With a good telescope, it was possible to make out vehicles and cattle moving up the hill towards Prescot, and occasionally, on a clear day, Black Combe, in Cumberland, was also visible. Today the name Mark Street still exists but the old houses have been demolished.

St. Domingo Mere, Everton, c.1858.
Herdman Collection 166.

The artist of this view is not named, but it is probably either W. G. Herdman or his son, William, who both lived in the Everton area and must have been familiar with this scene. St. Domingo Pit, or Mere, was on the corner of Mere Lane and Breckfield Road North, formerly known as Hangfield Lane. Stonehouse describes the Mere as a 'pretty and picturesque object, when seen with the morning sun upon the pretty trees that skirted its western bank', which is very much as it appears in this view. However he does add that 'it certainly did not smell very sweet at times.' In 1896 the 1_ acres occupied by the pond were acquired by Liverpool Corporation, drained and made into a recreation ground at a cost of £430.

This view in Everton shows houses near the junction of Rupert Lane, Everton Village and Everton Road. In the eighteenth and early nineteenth century Everton was a quiet rural area, with fresh air and extensive views, before

it began to attract Liverpool's wealthy merchants. These two houses have date stones of 1734, on the left, and 1735, on the right, as well as the name 'Thos Heys' and presumably his initials, 'T.H.'. Thomas Heyes of Everton is referred to in a rate assessment book dated 1705-8 owning land in the Everton area, as well as in Tithebarn Street in the centre of Liverpool.

Spekeland Road, Edge Hill, 1911.
F. Beattie, Beattie Collection 201.

These houses are part of group often known as Spekefield Cottages, just to the south of the Edge Hill railway sidings, off Spekeland Road. The cottages were built by a local landowner, John Shaw Leigh; work on them commenced in 1846 and they were originally intended for workers on the adjacent railways. Each cottage was built at the end of a long garden, some of which had greenhouses, around what was in effect a quadrangle. They provided quite a contrast with the densely packed terrace houses in the surrounding streets, all of which just had small back yards. By 1911 only five of the residents in the 63 houses had occupations obviously related to the railways, such as shunter or plate layer; other occupations included teacher of music, carter, book keeper, locksmith or labourer. J.A. Picton describes the houses as a 'sub-urban Eden', a 'rus in urbe', with 'the pretty effect of the cluster of gardens in the summer, blooming with flowers'.

F BEATTIE. 1911

Wavertree Park, Edge Lane, 1911.
F. Beattie, Beattie Collection 277.

This is the entrance to Wavertree Park at the junction of Edge Lane and Botanic Road. The site was originally occupied by an old house, surrounded by a grove of elms, named Plumbe's Hall after the family which lived there up to the early nineteenth century. In 1843 the Corporation purchased the land for £10,000 as the potential site for a new borough goal; however after the mansion had been demolished, the area was deemed unsuitable and it remained empty and abandoned for some years. In the 1850s as the movement for the creation of public parks in the city grew it was decided to lay out the land, at 'moderate expense' to form a new park, adjacent to the Botanic Gardens, which opened in 1856. Although small compared with other city parks, at only twenty four acres, it proved to be very popular in an area with little open space; band concerts on summer Thursday evenings were particularly popular, attracting large crowds.

Liverpool's first Botanic Gardens, founded in 1802 by William Roscoe, were situated on land in Myrtle Street. As the town expanded they were eventually surrounded on all sides by houses and in 1836 they moved to a new site in Edge Lane, shown here, which was purchased by the Corporation five years later. As well as maintaining a scientific collection, the Gardens were laid out in a series of colourful parterres. The glasshouses, which can be seen above the perimeter wall, were sadly bombed during World War II, but the Greek revival entrance lodge, on the far right of the picture, still stands on a much altered and busier Edge Lane.

F. Beattie 26/8/11

In August 1911 the Liverpool area was in the grip of a general transport strike, involving seamen, dockers, carters, railwaymen and others, after the escalation of a series of disputes. A demonstration on St George's Plateau on 13 August, involving an estimated 80-90,000 people, led to baton charges by troops and police,

Camp of the Northumberland Fusiliers on ground adjoining Wavertree Park, 1911.
F. Beattie, Beattie Collection 287.

who had been brought from other areas of the country. This picture, unlike most other views in this book, is specifically dated, 26th August 1911, and shows the Northumberland Fusiliers,

stationed in Liverpool in case of further trouble. They are depicted camped on land at the rear of Edge Lane Hall, where the former Littlewoods building stands today, and in the distance are the kennels and house associated with the Liverpool Dogs' Home, founded in 1883 and moved to Edge Lane in 1904.

Edge Lane, 1910.
F. Beattie, Beattie Collection 267.

This elegant row of houses, with its own driveway and gardens, called Fairfield Terrace, stood between Deane Road and Beech Street. In the 1860s the houses were home to a silk mercer, a merchant, a gentleman and a doctor of divinity, and in 1911 a coal merchant and a charcoal manufacturer. By the 1950s they had fallen into disrepair and were partly occupied by the firm of Holt's, who manufactured and sold the tiled fireplaces popular at that date. The terrace was finally demolished in the 1960s and the land used to extend the Taverner's sweet factory, which had premises to the rear in Beech Street.

Edge Lane Hall, 1909.
F. Beattie, Beattie Collection 35.

This building, which from its style may have dated back from the seventeenth century, stood on Edge Lane, where the Art Deco Littlewood's building was constructed in the 1938. In the 1820s and 30s it was owned by John Shaw Leigh, a Liverpool lawyer and important land owner in the area. The house was large, with seventeen bedrooms and extensive cellars and this, perhaps coupled with its age and rather gloomy appearance, gave rise to a number of stories of secret passages and haunted rooms. In 1886, on land adjacent to the hall, the grandly named International Exhibition of Navigation, Travel, Commerce and Manufacture, locally known as The Shipperies, was held; opened by Queen Victoria, it attracted over 3 million visitors, but despite this was a financial failure. The hall was demolished in 1913 to make an entrance for a later exhibition.

These detached houses, to the east of the junction of Edge Lane and Laurel Road, were two of a number of detached and semi-detached quality houses in this desirable area. In 1911 the Misses Penelope and Jessie

Edge Lane, 1910.
F. Beattie, Beattie Collection 269.

Graham lived at number 317 and Benjamin Edward Mercer at number 319, next to South

Bank Road. Laurel Motors Ltd. was established on the corner of Laurel Road in 1936 and Garthowen Road built on the site of the houses. Today the garage has gone and the site is empty, awaiting redevelopment.

OLD SWAN, BROADGREEN AND CHILDWALL

In the eighteenth century the area around Old Swan was only sparsely populated, with much of the area covered in moss and moorland. The land was owned by the Walton family and the name, Old Swan, is taken from their coat of arms, which depicted three swans on a blue shield. Local roads were only passable by horse, with Old Swan on the pack horse route to leading to Prescot. From the middle of the century it became an important junction for stage coach passengers, with coaches travelling to London via Broadgreen Road (formerly Petticoat Lane), and to Prescot, Wigan and east Lancashire via Prescot Road. Three inns were established, each, somewhat confusingly, called The Swan and known locally as the Old, Middle and Lower Swans. The area is actually shown as 'Old Swans', in the plural, on Yates and Perry's map of 1768. One of these inns, the 'Old Swan', at the junction of Prescot Road and Broadgreen Road, became the stopping place for coaches, as well as serving as the local post office.

The hamlet of Broadgreen (or Broad Green) was centred on the junction of Thomas Lane, Petticoat Lane (later Broad Green Road, now Bowring Park Road) and Rocky Lane (Score Lane). The roads in this area have changed both their names and routes over the years. The Broadgreen Abbey Hotel, built in 1848, stood at the junction and replaced former coaching inns known as the Bull's Head Inn and later the Bull and Railway Hotel. Broadgreen had its own railway station, on the original Liverpool to Manchester Railway, and Post Office, run for many years by the Jump family. The area is now overshadowed by the flyover of the M62 motorway constructed in the 1970s. Liverpool Garden Suburb, now more usually known as Wavertree Garden Suburb, is situated to the east of Wavertree High Street and was built on an area of land leased by the Liverpool Garden Suburb Tenants Ltd. Their aim was 'to provide a residential suburb for the people of Liverpool amid surroundings which conduce both health and pleasure.' The first house, in Wavertree Nook Road, was built in 1910 and there were also plenty of open spaces, with tree planted verges and recreational facilities. Childwall, centred on its parish church of All Saints, is another ancient parish, also mentioned in Domesday. At one time the parish, which included ten townships, covered over 16,000 acres, including 4,500 acres of foreshore on the River Mersey. The parish registers are some of the oldest on Merseyside, beginning in 1557. Childwall Hall once stood close to the church, amongst what were then extensive beech woods, with breathtaking views across south Lancashire. In the eighteenth century it was the home of two generations of Bamber Gascoynes, with the daughter and heiress of the second Bamber Gascoyne marrying the Marquis of Salisbury in 1821, uniting the extensive estates of both families. At the end of the nineteenth century Childwall was still a small village, with few dwellings besides the hall and the houses clustered around the church. In the 1930s many semi-detached houses were built on the land between Wavertree and Childwall and in the 1950s and 60s the valley overlooked by the church was also built on.

Thomas Lane, Knotty Ash, 1910.
F. Beattie, Beattie Collection 33.

This is Oak House at number 76 Thomas Lane and Beattie reproduces the date stone of 1782 over the centre window, although whose initials these are remain a mystery. The house has, for many years, been the home of the comedian Ken Dodd, who has made Knotty Ash famous for its mythical jam butty mines. In the distance is the spire of St. John the Evangelist Church, built 1835-7 of red ashlar, with the chancel added in 1890. When this picture was painted Thomas Lane curved to the left beyond the house to join Prescot Road, but today the line of the road continues straight ahead along Brookside Avenue.

F. BEATTIE 1911

Black Horse Smithy, Prescot Road, Old Swan, 1911.
F. Beattie, Beattie Collection 31.

The Black Horse smithy stood on the south side of Prescot Road, nearly opposite Black Horse Lane (formerly called Black Moss Lane) and in 1911 when this picture was painted it presents a pleasant rural scene, with little traffic to disturb the blacksmith's work, which has spilled onto the road outside. This section of Prescot Road once formed part of an old packhorse route from Liverpool to Prescot. The last proprietor of pack horses in south Lancashire, named Davies, kept one hundred horses at his stables in Old Swan. In the early years of the twentieth century Black Horse was still a distinct hamlet with a small group of cottages, an inn and the blacksmith's shown here. It is now just part of Old Swan and a Black Horse Inn still exists, on the north side of Prescot Road. The Regent cinema, which opened in 1926 on the site of the smithy, at the corner of Baden Road and Prescot Road, has now been replaced by flats and a supermarket.

Swan Row, Prescot Road, 1911.
F. Beattie, Beattie Collection 294.

Swan Row stood on the south side of Prescot Road, near its junction with Broadgreen Road. The front rooms of this row of small terrace houses were converted into shops to serve the growing neighbourhood. At this date rows of terrace housing were being built on either side of Prescot Road, including Baden, Leinster, Ulster, Munster and Belfast Roads to the south, and Dovercliffe, Southgate, Sunbeam, Orleans and Fitzgerald Roads to the north. This row survived until the 1960s, when they were demolished and replaced by modern shops. On the gable wall at the end of the row is an advertisement for 'Lewiss'(sic) tailoring', founded by David Lewis, which grew into the department store Lewis's at the corner of Ranelagh and Renshaw Streets.

Oak Hill Park, a group of about 25 Victorian villas, was situated off the west side of Broad Green Road, originally called Petticoat Lane. The area took its name from a number of mature oak trees which were removed and replanted there from the 'Ladies Walk', in Old Hall Street, during the construction of the

Junction of Broad Green Road and Oak Hill Road, 1912.
F. Beattie, Beattie Collection 292.

Leeds and Liverpool Canal. This picture shows Oaklands, which stood in its own grounds opposite All Saints Church. William E. Nelson, a cattle salesman lived there in the 1890s and

in the early years of the twentieth century it was owned by Samuel Robinson, who had worked his way up through the company to become managing director of the brewers Greenall Whitley. Today many of the villas have been demolished to make way for flats and modern houses.

F. BEATTIE. 1910

Oak Vale Cottages, Broadgreen, 1910.
F. Beattie, Beattie Collection 41.

This small group of cottages stood on Broadgreen Road, adjacent to where the Gardener's Arms public house stands today. The building in the centre is the original public house, with a lamp over the door and possibly advertising 'Walker's noted ales'. Both the houses and the public house took their names from a famous nursery, Oak Vale Nursery, which occupied all the land bordered by the present day Broadgreen Road, Warnerville Road and Sturdee Road. George Cunningham started his nursery in 1820 and the firm specialised in supplying trees and shrubs to estates in Britain and America. He was also one of the first nurserymen to introduce dahlias to this country. When he discovered that the line of the new Liverpool and Manchester Railway would run through his land he expressed great fears that his plants would be damaged by the resulting smoke and vibrations. However assurances were given and the nearby railway bridge was lavishly decorated with scarlet dahlias for the opening ceremony. By the time this picture was painted the nursery had closed, but the proprietor is remembered in nearby Cunningham Road. Between the houses was a footpath which followed the line of Edge Lane Drive, now Thomas Drive, to its junction with Thomas Lane.

Broadgreen Road, 1910.
F. Beattie, Beattie Collection 42.

This view shows what was probably the original public house at the junction known locally as 'The Rocket'; today it is the site of Rockville Road, opposite the Queens Drive flyover. Beattie reproduces the 1739 date stone, with the initials 'W.E.', from the thatched building. There is some uncertainty as to just how many public houses there have been on this site. Hoult in his history of the area refers to a pub in the vicinity being given the name Rocket to attract the custom of navvies working on the nearby Liverpool to Manchester Railway in the late 1820s, but the six inch to one mile Ordnance Survey map of the area, published in 1851, shows a Railway Tavern, rather than a Rocket.

In 1889 a new brick-built pub opened on the opposite side of the road, which stood until the 1970s when it was demolished to make way for the M62 motorway. By 1919 the old cottage was tenanted by John Shinkfield, proprietor of Broad Green Dairy Farm. The barn, at right-angles to the cottage, was demolished in 1914 when the road was widened for trams, but the cottage remained until 1920.

Rocky Lane Farm, 1910.
F. Beattie, Beattie Collection 246.

Until the early 1930s Rocky Lane was, as its name suggests, still a country lane, sunk between sandstone walls and hedges. It ran from Priory Road (now Queens Drive), and from this junction followed a route slightly north of where it is today. Its junction with Score Lane, then little more than a footpath, was close to where Durston Road has been built. Rocky Lane Farm was situated on the east side of Rocky Lane, north of its junction with Score Lane, and had been farmed by the Pye family for nearly ninety years before its demolition to make way for housing. In 1865 Thomas Pye was the tenant, with much of the land in the area owned by the Lords of Salisbury. Mrs. Sarah Pye was tenant of Rocky Lane Farm in 1911, but by 1936 semi-detached houses had been built there and the farm was no more.

Broad Green Farm, Rocky Lane, 1910.
F. Beattie, Beattie Collection 249.

Broad Green Farm was situated further along Rocky Lane, closer to its junction with Broad Green Road, now Bowring Park Road and for some time this farm was also worked by members of the Pye family, cousins of those at Rocky Lane Farm. As early as 1869 the Marquis of Salisbury advertised building land in the area to let on a 99 year lease, but it was not until the 1930s that building really started. Many of the houses were originally built for rent on 999 year leases, but have subsequently been purchased. One of the major builders was Mrs. F. Ebbs, director of Celebrated Ebbs Houses Ltd., who described herself as 'Liverpool's woman builder'. A number of new roads were also built at this time, including Bentham Drive and Bowland Avenue.

The small group of cottages, known as Moss Cottages, stood at the junction of Wavertree Nook Road and Thingwall Road, previously known as Kettle Nook. This area was incorporated into the Liverpool Garden Suburb, now usually referred to as Wavertree Garden Suburb, planned as part of the garden suburb movement in the early years of the twentieth century. An area of land was leased to The

Wavertree Nook Road, 1910.
F. Beattie, Beattie Collection 233.

Liverpool Garden Suburb Tenants Ltd., whose aim was to build houses, at the low density of just 10 to12 per acre instead of the more usual 40, all with bathrooms and their own gardens. Recreational facilities such as tennis courts, a bowling green and playgrounds were also

provided. The foundation stone of the first house on the estate, in Wavertree Nook Road, was laid in 1910. It was originally intended that the estate should reach as far north as the railway line to Manchester, on the far side of Queens Drive, but work was halted by World War I and never resumed. Here we are looking south across fields towards the chimneys of the Dudlow Lane Pumping Station.

This tranquil scene depicts Priory Road, between present day Thingwall Road and Childwall Road, now Queens Drive, looking south towards Childwall. In the distance, to the right, the chimneys of the Dudlow Lane Pumping station are again visible, and on the left are the white buildings of the farm called Childwall Priory. Queens Drive was conceived

Priory Road, 1910.
F. Beattie, Beattie Collection 237.

by John Brodie, Liverpool's City Engineer, in the early 1900s and when completed provided a seven mile circular route from the north to the south of the city, avoiding congested areas and passing through what was then undeveloped

agricultural land. The section built along the route of Priory Road was a dual carriageway and had a wide central reservation planted with trees. Brodie's foresight in the early years of the twentieth century means that the same road can still cope with today's enormously increased volume of traffic.

61

F. BEATTIE, 1910

**Junction of Childwall Road
and Childwall Priory Road, 1910.**
F. Beattie, Beattie Collection 242.

In the early years of the century, when Beattie painted this view, looking northwards, Childwall Road and Childwall Priory Road were just tracks across fields, and there was so little traffic that there was even a grassy mound in the centre of the junction. Today that grassy mound has been replaced by the large roundabout, known as Childwall Fiveways, on one of the busiest routes through the city. The Childwall section of Queens Drive was built

shortly after this picture was painted, when Childwall Priory Road was converted to a dual carriageway as part of the new 'circumferential boulevard', which continued across the junction on its route south towards Sefton Park. The gate leads to Childwall Priory farm, which, until its demolition in the early 1930s,

stood on the site of the present day Paignton and Orton Roads. There had been a farm here for over 500 years, but the church-like additions made to one end of the farm buildings in the 1820s may have given rise to its final name, and despite evidence from local place names, such as 'abbey' and 'priory', opinion is divided over whether there ever was a religious house in the area.

All Saints' Church, Childwall, 1912.
F. Beattie, Beattie Collection 245.

The ancient parish of Childwall was referred to in the Domesday Book and covered a large area which extended to Hale and Halewood in the east and included Garston, Wavertree, Allerton, and Much and Little Woolton. All Saints' Church, built of local red sandstone, still has some fourteenth century masonry, although there have been many later additions and alterations. A chapel for Isaac Green, of

Childwall Hall, was built in the eighteenth century and in 1810-11, after fears about its stability, the tower was rebuilt to its original design. In the early nineteenth century a crenellated 'hearse house' was built by the road, and in this picture almost appears to be

part of the church. Score Lane, from where this view is taken, was one of the oldest roads on the outskirts of Liverpool and may have taken its name from the old English for a common field. However although it had once been a right of way, by the early twentieth century, as shown here, it was closed with gates across it, marked private and only open to pedestrians and cyclists.

Childwall Cottages, Childwall Lane, 1952.
A.H. Jones, A.H. Jones Collection 169.

The area of Childwall around the church, even today, retains its village atmosphere. Childwall's All Saints Church is Liverpool's only surviving medieval church and its peaceful churchyard looks out across the south Lancashire plain from its position high on a sandstone ridge. These cottages, also known as Tower Yard, used to stand opposite the junction of Childwall Lane (not Childwall Road as indicated in the painting) and Well Lane. James Hoult, the local historian, writing in the early twentieth century, suggests that they were built as almshouses, but frustratingly does not give a source for his information. However, with their arched doorway, echoed in the detailing of the stonework above, they do not appear to be standard workmen's cottages. An early photograph suggests that the roof was once crenellated, in a similar fashion to that of the Childwall Abbey public house, the hearse house at the church and the adjacent Childwall Hall. At the far end of the yard was a columbarium or dovecote, later converted into a house. The cottages were demolished to make way for the Alice Elliot School for the Deaf, whose entrance now occupies the site.

WAVERTREE

Wavertree, now a suburb of Liverpool, was once just a village, four miles from the centre of Liverpool; however even today it retains a distinct identity. The settlement of Wavertree is very old; in the mid-nineteenth century workmen discovered ancient burial urns in the area of Sandown Park and it is referred to in the Domesday Book as Wauretree. Monks Well, north of the village green, provided water for the area and is thought to be of great antiquity, although no connection with a monastic community has been proved. In the mid-eighteenth century the large area of Wavertree Green was used as common pasture. The Township of Wavertree developed slowly at first, with a population of just 290 in 1731, but by 1901, six years after it was incorporated into the city of Liverpool, this had reached 25,300. Wavertree is still centred on the High Street and a number of Georgian houses survive, with Victorian and Edwardian civic buildings, a mixture of smaller terraced houses off the main road, and Victorian villas in Sandown and Victoria Parks.

Rathbone Road, 1910.
F. Beattie, Beattie Collection 203.

The spire of St. Mary's Church is clearly visible in this view, looking north west from the junction of Rathbone Road and Long Lane. The church was built in the 1850s but destroyed by bombing in World War II. It was situated in Sandown Park, a small residential estate laid out in 'picturesque' style in the 1840s by the architect Cornelius Sherlock in the grounds of Sandown Hall. The houses of the estate can be seen in the distance. Today just a few semi-detached villas remain: Sandown Hall was sadly demolished in 2000 and much of the area is occupied by modern housing. The large house to the left of the picture was Lenaghmore, occupied by in 1901 by Mary Cullen, a single woman of independent means, with her housekeeper, housemaid and kitchenmaid. One of the original lodges of Sandown Hall can be seen just in front of Lenaghmore.

High Street, Wavertree, 1946.
A.H. Jones, A.H. Jones Collection 18.

These three old cottages stood on the north side of the High Street, at numbers 47 to 51. They were built of brick, with stone or slate roofs, which appear in the painting to be original, and the two on the right had a low sandstone wall in front of small gardens. The left-hand cottage has had a small shop built onto the front. In the late 1940s they were occupied, from left to right, by Mrs Jessie Stewart, a wardrobe dealer (not someone who buys and sells wardrobes, but a second-hand clothes dealer), Joseph Birch, a labourer, and Mrs Elizabeth McGuirk. To the right is The Rose public house, licensee Andrew Murphy, which still survives. In the early years of the twentieth century a blacksmith's premises was squeezed in the small space behind the cottages. They were demolished in 1969 and the site is now a small public garden named the Rose Garden.

ALFRED·H·JONES·

This shop still stands at number 102 Wavertree High Street, on the left hand side of the road looking towards the centre of Liverpool, just beyond Wavertree Clock Tower. It is one of a small group of late Georgian buildings and, interestingly, still retains its early nineteenth century shop front. When A. H. Jones painted this view the premises were occupied by Mrs. Florence Whittaker and George Hampton, a boot repairer, and at number 102A were William Jones and Son, cabinet makers. Traces of all these can be seen in the picture. In 1978 it was still a cobbler's, but today is, appropriately, occupied by a woodworker.

At number 4 Church Road (now Church Road North), this house was occupied in 1949 by Ernest Findley Jenkins and today is the premises of B. Jenkins, funeral directors. The

Corner of High Street and Church Road, Wavertree, 1946.
A.H. Jones, A.H. Jones Collection 19.

house appears old but is difficult to date due to later alterations. The black and white timber effect has been painted on and is still there today.

Anderton Square, 1911.
F. Beattie, Beattie Collection 210.

This small group of houses was set back from the south side of Wavertree High Street, opposite the Police Station. In the early years of the twentieth century there were a number of similar small squares and yards off this side of the High Street, with much of the property, as suggested in this view, being very small and of poor quality. At this date the five cottages were occupied by a Corporation labourer, a groom, a railway engine driver, a tram driver (with two lodgers) and a widow and her son, who was a shop porter. They were eventually demolished in the 1930s to make way for the flats of Wavertree Gardens built by the Corporation and designed by Sir Lancelot Keay, which have now been converted to private apartments called Abbeygate.

Childwall Road, 1910.
F. Beattie, Beattie Collection 55.

This group of buildings stood on the north-east corner of the junction of Childwall Road and Mill Road. To the left is Yew Tree House, and although the buildings to the right appear to be considerably older it is not clear which house the date stone reproduced by Beattie came from. The Plumbe family owned a considerable amount of property in the Liverpool area and this connection continued for 250 years, with Thomas Plumbe being the last family member to live here. By the time this picture was painted John Dilworth, a local builder, who also had works in Chatham Street, was the occupier of Yew Tree House.

**Wavertree Old Stile Road,
off Prince Alfred Road, 1909.**
F. Beattie, Beattie Collection 51.

Old Stile Road was actually little more than a track which led from Prince Alfred Road, formerly known as Cow Lane, across fields to the south of Wavertree Playground to join Smithdown Road just before the railway bridge, the route now followed by Grant Avenue. Prince Alfred Road was probably renamed after the second son of Queen Victoria, who visited Wavertree in 1866. To the left are the gateposts of Field House, demolished shortly after this view was taken, to make way for the development of Grant Avenue.

Wavertree Green, 1910.
F. Beattie, Beattie Collection 47.

In the eighteenth century Wavertree Green covered 409 acres and was used as common pasture land. It extended from Monks' Well, on Mill Lane to Wavertree Nook in one direction and to Elm Hall, in Lance Lane, in the other. A private Act of Parliament, the Wavertree Enclosure Act of 1768, brought in by Bamber Gascoyne, M.P. for Liverpool and Lord of the Manor, divided the land into fields between himself and his tenants. A number of new roads including Thingwall Road and Church Road were laid out, and the remaining open space, bounded by Church Road, Woolton Road, Lance Lane and Childwall Road, is shown here, looking towards Woolton Road. An unusual condition of the Act was that no building on the Green should exceed 4 feet 6 inches in height and this restriction remained until 1937, when, amid much local opposition, houses and the Abbey cinema were built.

F. BEATTIE 1911

Wavertree Mill and quarry, 1911.
F. Beattie, Beattie Collection 48.

Wavertree Mill, seen in this and the previous view, was situated on the south side of Woolton Road, and its site can still be seen at the end of Charles Berrington Road. This was one of the so-called 'King's mills' and from 1475 to 1629 was owned by the reigning monarch. All tenants of the Manor of Wavertree were compelled to bring their corn to be ground at the 'King's mill' and were subject to penalties if they took it elsewhere. The rights of the mill were later sold to the Earl of Derby and then Bamber Gascoyne. The clause limiting the height of buildings in the Enclosure Act of 1768 was apparently to guarantee that the windmill was not obstructed in any way. By the nineteenth century restrictions on the use of the mill had been abolished and it was owned by Sir James Bourne. Windmills could be dangerous buildings; the son of Sir James's coachman was killed by one of the revolving sails and in another accident the miller's daughter was caught by the hair and scalped, although fortunately she survived. When Beattie painted the mill in 1911 its days were numbered and it was finally demolished in 1916.

F.BEATTIE, 1910

WILLIAM BUNCE
NURSERYMAN & FLORIST
FLOWERS & PLANTS ON SALE

Corner of Woolton Road and Church Road, Wavertree, 1910.
F. Beattie, Beattie Collection 217.

This picture, looking along Woolton Road, shows the houses in Brereton Avenue, built in the early twentieth century, and a signpost indicating the route to Gateacre and Woolton. A notice advertises the nursery of William Bunce, 'nurseryman and florist: flowers and plants on sale'. His nursery ran alongside Church Road as far the present day Beverley Road and Brereton Road was probably built on part of the nursery. He also had a florist's shop at number 36 High Street and more nursery land in Prince Alfred Road, between Paradise Gardens and Anderton Square. At the junction is what appears to be a drinking fountain and to the far right, on the pavement, beyond the seat, is a mounting block, which is still there today.

F. BEATTIE 1910

Holy Trinity Church, Church Road, Wavertree, 1910.
F. Beattie, Beattie Collection 219.

Holy Trinity Church was built in Neoclassical style by John Hope in 1794 as a chapel of ease to All Saints', Childwall and in 1911, shortly after this picture was painted, a chancel was added to the east end by Charles Reilly. In the 1950s the tower was found to be structurally weak, possibly due to the effects of bombing during World War II. The top portion, together with the cupola, were removed, leaving just the square base, and have never been rebuilt. Despite major fires in 1961 and 1971, caused by vandalism, the church has been restored and celebrated its bi-centenary in 1994. The large churchyard contains the graves of Wavertree residents spanning more than 200 years, from when it was just a small village to a suburb of today's large city.

Dunbabin Farm, 1910.
F. Beattie, Beattie Collection 54.

Looking eastwards, this shows the farm which stood at the junction of Dunbabin Road and Woolton Road. In 1841 John Dunbabin, a farmer, and his unmarried sister Mary, also a farmer, lived here in Woolton Road, and, although they had retired, they were still there in 1861. The farm and subsequently the road both took their name from the family. Today the area to the left of the picture is occupied by Mosspits Lane Schools.

On the left is the Halfway House public house, licensee in 1946 John Pierpoint Brown, which is still there today. To the right is the Dudlow Lane Pumping Station, the chimneys of which formed a landmark visible from many places in the area and shown in several pictures in this book. In the mid 1860s Liverpool was suffering from a severe shortage of water, due to increased population and drought conditions, so that it was only possible to provide water for two hours each day.

The towers and engine house, built out of local red sandstone, stood over a well, 257 feet deep, with two shafts and boreholes at its base, capable of pumping one million gallons of water each day. A small group of cottages was constructed on the site to house workers. In 1872 questions were raised about the purity of the water obtained from this source, as it was thought that sewage from cesspits adjoining a number of large houses in the area was leaking into the wells, and a number of sewers were built to remedy the problem. The buildings continued in use for nearly one hundred years until their demolition in 1950, although a covered reservoir on the site remained. Today the flats of Dudlow Mansions stand on the site of the workers' cottages and new retirement apartments are being built on the site of the pumping station.

AROUND SEFTON PARK

Sefton Park, at nearly 270 acres, is Liverpool's largest park, described in the city's 'Handbook to Parks' in 1905 as 'one of the finest public parks in the world'. In 1863 the Corporation had resolved that 'it is desirable to provide Parks and other spaces for the public...' and a site was purchased form the Earl of Sefton. Many features included in the original plan, such as a grand conservatory, Moorish kiosks, windmills, archery and cricket grounds and aviaries, had to be modified due to the escalating costs. However the park did eventually acquire its grand conservatory when the Palm House, a gift of Henry Yates Thompson, opened in 1896. An article in the 'Liverpool Echo' published in 1930 described the area around Aigburth and Sefton Park as once having a 'countrified aspect' and regretted the change in character brought about by arterial roads and increasing numbers of new suburban houses. The Aigburth area had begun to attract prosperous Liverpool merchants in the early nineteenth century and many large houses were built, with their own grounds and lodges, and cottages for servants. By the end of the century public transport had brought this area within easy reach of the centre of Liverpool and some of the old estates were broken up, with the land sold to speculative builders who constructed rows of terraced housing. However some parts retained their distinctive character, including St. Michael's Hamlet, to the south of Aigburth Road, and Otterspool, until the mid nineteenth century a fishing hamlet on the banks of the River Mersey.

F. BEATTIE 1910

Eastfield, Sefton Park Road, 1910.
F. Beattie, Beattie Collection 125.

Lodge Lane originally extended south to join Ullet Road opposite the entrance to Sefton Park, but in 1908 this section was renamed Sefton Park Road. This large detached house stood opposite the end of Bentley Road, between Grove Park and Fern Grove. In 1901 the house was occupied by Col. Henry Wainwright, a marble and cement merchant, born in Canada in 1847, together with his wife Eliza, sons Richard and Henry, daughters Ellen, Elizabeth, Hilda and Mary, and their cook, housemaid and waitress. Today the site is occupied by modern low-rise flats.

F BEATTIE 1910

Corner of Sefton Park Road and Grove Park, 1910.
F. Beattie, Beattie Collection 124.

Lodge Lane took its name from the supposed site of a hunting lodge dating from the days when Toxteth Park was a royal hunting park for King John. According to James Picton Lodge Lane benefited from its proximity to Prince's Park, where high quality housing had been built to fund the layout of the park, and this ancient road was 'very early formed into a pleasant suburb'. A map of 1768 shows seven villas already built along the road and in 1852 work started on the construction of Grove Park, which formed a cul de sac of semi-detached villas with gardens, most of which still remain.

Elms House, Ullet Road, 1910.
F. Beattie, Beattie Collection 120.

This house stood adjacent to the tramway sheds, which can just be seen to the left, at the town end of Ullet Road, near its junction with Park Road and Aigburth Road. In 1907, when Robert Griffiths was writing his history of Toxteth Park, the house was the home of Mrs. Williston, who had lived there since 1848. Efforts were apparently being made by the Corporation and a number of brewers and other firms, to persuade her to sell what would have been a valuable site. It would appear from the 'for sale' notices in this picture that their efforts had been successful, but the garden still appears to be there in 1927, although by 1953 the entire site had been covered by a bus depot. In the garden of the house, behind the wall to the right, were six ancient elm trees, which gave their name to both the house and the road beside it leading to Peel Street. Today the bus depot has gone and the area is covered by the houses of Mallins Close.

This house, Holly Bank, stands at the junction of St. Michael's Road and St. Michael's Church Road, opposite Bryanston Road, in a small area known as St. Michael's Hamlet. This small group of five stuccoed villas and the church of St. Michael-in-the-Hamlet were the work of John Cragg, proprietor of the Mersey Iron Foundry, and were built in the early years of the nineteenth century. As might have been expected much use was made of iron in the construction of both the church and the houses. Holly Bank was John Cragg's own house, adjoining the churchyard, with a large garden, stables and a coach house. The elaborate Gothic gates on the left lead to the garden, with the large coach house door in the centre and the entrance to the stables beyond. In its early years the church served a wide area and parishioners, who travelled long distances on horseback, stabled their horses here during services. A few additional villas were built in the 1840s, but by the 1880s the character of the area changed completely as terraced houses were built on all sides of the hamlet.

Sefton Park Lake, 1944.
A.H. Jones, A.H. Jones Collection 4.

Sefton Park, officially opened by Prince Arthur, Duke of Connaught, in 1872, was Liverpool's most prestigious park, situated in the wealthier southern part of the city and intended for the area's respectable residents. The Corporation purchased the land for the park and a public competition held to determine the design was won by Edouard André, Gardener in Chief for Paris, who was responsible for the layout and landscaping, and Lewis Hornblower, a Liverpool architect, who designed the park buildings. Features in the park included an archery field and cricket ground, an iron bridge, a bandstand, the Palm House and the lake, shown here, where for many years rowing boats were available to hire and model yacht regattas were held. Building plots around the edge of the park, for the construction of private villas, were sold to help finance the park's construction.

84

F.BEATTIE 1910

The entrance to Sefton Park is just to the right of this view, which looks north-westwards along Aigburth Road. The villas of Fulwood Park, one of a number of private residential estates built in Liverpool in the nineteenth century, can be seen through the trees on the left. Work on this

Aigburth Road,
near Sefton Park gates, 1910.
F. Beattie, Beattie Collection 138.

particular estate started in the 1840s and it consisted of a single road, entered via a lodge and gates, leading down to the River Mersey,

with about 20 large villas, in secluded gardens built on either side. Although there is little evidence in this picture Aigburth Road was one of the main tramway routes out of Liverpool, with the tram track running down the centre of the road.

F BEATTIE 1912

Roselands, Woodlands Road, 1912.
F. Beattie, Beattie Collection 143.

This appears to be the lodge or cottage adjacent to the house called Roselands, rather than the actual house. In 1907 it was occupied by William Radcliffe, who, after he retired from business in 1878, became was involved in politics and a number of Liverpool associations. After being elected a town councillor in 1878, he served as mayor in 1882-3 and was made an alderman in 1889. He became president of the Liverpool Law Society, honorary treasurer of the Liverpool Constitutional Association and a governor of the Blue Coat School. On the lighter side, he was a member of the Royal Mersey Yacht Club and exhibited prize winning chrysanthemums. Today the site is occupied by houses.

F. BEATTIE 1912

Kelton, Woodlands Road, 1912.
F. Beattie, Beattie Collection 144.

The original stuccoed villa of Kelton was built in the early nineteenth century, but a large Victorian Gothic extension was added in the 1860s and the lodge, shown here, matches this style. Joshua Sing, a leather dealer with the family firm of Powell and Sing, lived there in the early twentieth century and the 1901 census shows that as well as his wife, Florentia, and daughter, Edith, there were a cook, parlour maid, lady's maid, two housemaids, an under housemaid and a kitchenmaid. Like William Radcliffe he was a governor of the Blue Coat School, but he was also involved in other educational work, including acting as chairman of the managers of the North Corporation Board School and a member of the Liverpool Council of Education, as well as founding a scholarship for girls. However his hobby, meteorology, formed quite a contrast to his educational work. The house later became a convent, with a chapel added in 1925, and then, with even more additions to the building, a care home. Today the house is sadly empty and derelict, with the grounds occupied by social housing and a church hall.

The tower of the church of St. Matthew and St. James, Mossley Hill's parish church, situated on a sandstone ridge 188 feet above sea level, has dominated the south Liverpool skyline since its building in the 1870s. Funded by a visitor to Mossley Hill, who declared it 'a wonderful site for a church', it is dedicated to the saints after whom he was named. Designed by Paley and

Mossley Hill Church, 1949.
Allan P. Tankard, Binns Collection C266.

Austin of Lancaster, the early parishioners from its mostly rural parish consisted of wealthy merchants and their servants from the nearby big houses and the church memorials were described by a local historian as 'a microcosm of

Liverpool's upper strata of society in late Victorian and Edwardian times'. However in the twentieth century the area changed as the surrounding fields were gradually covered with houses. Although not apparent in this view, in August 1940 the church was severely damaged in one of Liverpool's first air raids and restoration work continued until 1953.

Carnatic Hall, 1947.
Allan P. Tankard, Binns Collection C193.

Carnatic Hall, in Elmswood Road, was built in the eighteenth century, on the site of one of the earliest houses in the area, by Peter Baker, who made a fortune from his activities as a privateer. He built a ship called the Mentor, described as 'a sorry specimen of a ship, clumsy, ill-built, lopsided … with sailing qualities more suited to a haystack than a smart privateer', rejected by its prospective owner, Baker equipped the 'Mentor' himself. A month after sailing from Liverpool in September 1778, his ship captured an unarmed French East Indiaman, the Carnatic, which had a cargo including a box of diamonds valued at between £135,00 and £400,000. His house was subsequently named Carnatic Hall by local wits, although the name does not appear to have been formally used until 1889. During World War II Liverpool Museum used the house for the storage of museum exhibits away from the centre of the city. The house was demolished in 1964 and it is now the site of Liverpool University's halls of residence, although the name has been preserved.

F. BEATTIE 1910

Otterspool Farm, Church Lane, Aigburth, 1910.
F. Beattie, Beattie Collection 81.

This farm, situated in a road named after the adjacent St. Anne's Church, was once owned by Sir Thomas Edwards-Moss and became the home of his farm bailiff. Thomas Moss was born at Otterspool in 1811 and after marrying Amy Charlotte Edwards, the daughter of Richard Edwards of Roby, assumed her name to become Thomas Edwards-Moss. He became a director of the North-Western Bank and chairman of the Liverpool Consitutional Association. However the coat of arms, shown over the upper window of the left-hand gable is not his, but belongs to William Clayton, M.P. and Mayor of Liverpool from 1689 to 1690, and his wife, Elizabeth Leigh. The site is now occupied by St. Margaret's Primary School and Mersey View Special School.

**Holmefield Road,
looking towards Aigburth Road, 1910.**
F. Beattie, Beattie Collection 147.

Holmefield Road ran through fields from the end of Booker's Lane, in the east, past several large villas, to Aigburth Road. This rural scene shows the straight, eastern section of the road, before it drops downhill to join the main road. On the crest of the hill, just out of sight here, stood the large house, named Holmefield, a square, stuccoed villa with an Ionic portico, built in the 1830s, which now, much altered, forms part of the I.M. Marsh campus of Liverpool John Moores University. Further along the road is Ivyhurst, a Victorian gothic villa, once the Grange Hotel which has now been converted into flats.

This is arguably the oldest inhabited building in Liverpool and, although much altered, still retains a three-light mullioned window and external stairs. The left hand part was known as the Granary and the section to the right, sadly demolished for road widening after World War I, the Monk's Lodging. It is believed that the

Stanlawe Grange, Aigburth Hall Road, 1909.
F. Beattie, Beattie Collection 67.

building, parts of which date from the late thirteenth century, originally served as a grange, or barn, for the monks of Stanlawe, on the opposite bank of the River Mersey in Cheshire.

The surviving building is of cruck frame construction, with massive local red sandstone walls, over three feet thick in places. Stonor in his book on Liverpool's early Catholic history suggests that the grange could have been used by local recusant families, such as the Tarletons and Harringtons, as a place of worship.

ALLERTON

The name Allerton probably means 'place of the alders' and evidence of early settlement here can be seen in the six Calderstones, thought to been part of a megalithic passage grave and carved with cup and ring motifs. They have been moved from their original site and are now in a glasshouse on the Hart Hill estate. Allerton was mentioned in the Domesday Book and in the twelfth and thirteenth centuries was a royal forest, with hunting, chasing and hawking under the jurisdiction of the Master Forester of West Derby. The Allerton Oak, in Calderstones Park, reputedly dates from this time, but although its base is ten feet in diameter, it is probably not that old. By the sixteenth century furze and heather covered much of the area, although the lower lying sections were probably farmed, and most of the land had been enclosed by the eighteenth century. However the population remained small, only 178 in 1801, and it was not until the nineteenth century that Allerton became an attractive residential area for Liverpool's merchants and businessmen. Prior to then most had lived above their business premises in town, but as roads improved and travel became easier, it was possible to live further afield. Large estates were held by influential families and a number of these survive as parks, such as Calderstones and Hart Hill and green open spaces like Allerton Golf Course. Today, despite much suburban development in the 1930s, Allerton remains a pleasant leafy area.

This narrow lane ran from Greenhill Road to Holmefield Road, crossing the London and North Western Railway line from Liverpool Lime Street, and is now known as Booker Avenue. The surrounding land formed part of the estate of Josias Booker, a West India merchant who had plantations in British Guiana, where he

Booker's Lane, 1911.
F. Beattie, Beattie Collection 80.

was noted for his concern for the welfare of his workers. His country residence, Poplar Grove, stood at the far end of Booker's Lane, near its junction with Holmefield Road and was one of

the oldest houses in the neighbourhood. With his brother George he founded the firm which became Booker McConnell and Co. Ltd. (of Booker prize fame). The cottages, which each had their own gardens, were built for his farm workers and stood on the north side of the lane until their demolition in 1936-7.

Booker's School, 1911.
F. Beattie, Beattie Collection 183.

Just beyond the cottages shown in the previous view was a small school for the education of 'poor children', founded by Josias Booker's daughter Margaret in 1861, which she ran at her own expense for a number of years. Her initials can be seen in the stone above the doorway and are reproduced by Beattie. In 1907 the schoolmistress was Miss M. Morgan. After the cottages and the little school were demolished Booker Avenue Junior and Infant School was built on the site and Booker's Lane became Booker Avenue, 'a fine modern arterial'.

This rural scene shows Rose Lane looking southwest from Allerton Road, with the tower of St. Matthew and St. James, Mossley Hill's parish church, in the distance, and the road gently rising to towards the bridge at Mossley

Hill Station. On the right hand side there are still open fields, but the houses of Rose Brae can be seen behind the trees to the left. Today the land in front of these houses is occupied by a large Tesco supermarket.

Smithdown Place, 1945.
A.H. Jones, A.H. Jones Collection 15.

This view of 1945 shows the tram terminus at the junction of Penny Lane, Smithdown Road and Church Road, known as Smithdown Place, with St. Barnabas Church on the left. The original church consisted of an iron chapel on Smithdown Road, which served as a chapel of ease to St. Matthew and St. James, Mossley Hill. As the population of the area increased a more permanent building was required and the site on Allerton Road was secured in 1911, with the new church consecrated on 21st February 1914. The low colonnaded building on the right featured on the Beatles single Penny Lane, released in 1967, and at that date served as a bus shelter, inspectors' office and public convenience. In the mid 1980s it opened as a Beatles themed café, Sgt. Pepper's, but plans to extend it by adding an upper floor were turned down in 2007. Today the café has closed, although Penny Lane still forms part of the Beatles tour.

**Junction of Allerton and
Limedale Roads, 1909.**
F. Beattie, Beattie Collection 169.

Although the road names in the painting are not legible information from other sources indicates that this is probably a view of Hillside Cottage, which stood at the junction of these two roads when Limedale Road was just a track. The conical structure in front of the house may be a beehive. In the 1920s this area of farmland was gradually covered in the semi-detached houses of Limedale, Mapledale and Rosedale Roads.

Menlove Avenue, 1911.
F. Beattie, Beattie Collection 150.

Menlove Avenue was constructed in 1910 to provide a link between the newly constructed Queens Drive, at its junction with Smithdown Road and Allerton Road, and the far end of Allerton Road, adjacent to Woolton village. Mendips at 251 Menlove Avenue was the childhood home of John Lennon. This picture looks north across fields from the western end of the road towards the towers of the Dudlow Lane pumping station in the distance. Several of the large, detached houses in Dudlow Lane are also visible and included Dudlow Grange, occupied by John H Dovener, a sack manufacturer, Dudlow House with the hide broker James E Gordon and Arthur Crosthwaite's house, Fylingside.

F. BEATTIE, 1910

In the 1840s Calderstones Road, as far as its junction with Harthill Road, was known as Spencer's Lane and beyond this, Allerton Lane. This view shows the old Allerton police station, occupied in 1881 by the local 'bobby' Patrick McGuiness, from Ireland, his wife and four children. The building may have stood close to the junction of Calderstones and Harthill Roads, but its precise location is not clear from either contemporary maps or census returns.

FRED BEATTIE, 1901

Calderstones Road, 1901.
F. Beattie, Beattie Collection 152.

This rural scene shows Calderstones Road looking north, from near its junction with Allerton Road, and in the distance is a small group of cottages where it joins Harthill Road.

Also at this junction was Hartfield, a detached, Italianate, stuccoed mansion built in the 1840s by Charles Wilson and bought by John Walmsley, a Liverpool shipowner in 1882. It formed the nucleus of Calder High School for girls and is now part of Calderstones School.

F BEATTIE 1910

Harthill Road, 1910.
F. Beattie, Beattie Collection 156.

This is the lodge to Quarry Bank, designed in 1866 by the architects Culshaw and Summers for the timber merchant James Bland. The house, in local dark sandstone, is built in a 'muscular Gothic' style, with an impressive wood panelled staircase, presumably reflecting Bland's professional interest in such matters, and stained glass windows. Its conspicuous tower gave it the local nickname 'Bland's Sawmills'. The lodge reflects the style of the main building, which is now, with Hartfield, part of Calderstones School.

102

This farm was situated in open fields between Greenhill Road and what is now the main railway line to London, an area now occupied by the Liverpool University athletic grounds. In 1835 it was owned by Edward Griffin, who also owned property approximately where Mossley Hill Station stands today. Then the seventy acres were farmed by Herbert Lucas and the land was mainly under meadow or pasture, with small quantities of carrots, potatoes and wheat also grown. In 1907, when this picture was painted, Samuel Lightfoot farmed the land and a path led westwards over fields to a footbridge crossing the railway line, which then headed southwards in the direction of Mossley Hill Road. Pittville Road, Avenue and Close, consisting of semi-detached houses typical of 1930s suburbia, are all named after the farm.

F. BEATTIE 1900

Allerton Road, 1900.
F. Beattie, Beattie Collection 171.

Bibby's Farm was probably situated on the east side of Allerton Road, close to its junction with Calderstones Road, although it is not named as such on contemporary maps. John Bibby, a Liverpool iron and copper merchant, who lived at nearby Hart Hill, built All Hallows Church as a memorial to his first wife Fanny, and the farm would have been known locally by this name. The picture shows a long, low sandstone building, with a wall in front and Calderstones Road leading off to the right. At this date Allerton Road is still just a rough track leading through farmland.

WOOLTON AND GATEACRE

Woolton, or Much Woolton, is the site of one of the oldest settlements in Liverpool. Camp Hill, still open land today, was once an Iron Age encampment, complete with ramparts, although the name 'Woolton' probably derives from the Anglo Saxon. From the fourteenth century until the dissolution of the monasteries by Henry VIII in the mid sixteenth century, the Manor of Woolton was granted to the Order of Hospitallers of St. John, a religious order who cared for sick pilgrims. Isaac Green, a Liverpool lawyer, acquired land in the area in the mid seventeenth century and it then passed, together with land in Childwall, through the daughter of Bamber Gascoyne, to the Marquis of Salisbury.

As with most villages on the outskirts of Liverpool, the population grew slowly, from just 175 in 1658 to 439 by 1801 and 4,750 at the end of the nineteenth century. The initial impetus for this growth stemmed from the 'Childwall and Woolton Waste Lands Inclosure Act' of 1805, which allowed the common land, used by locals for grazing, stone quarrying and marl digging, to be enclosed by walls or fences. In practice it particularly benefited local landowners, such as Bamber Gascoyne, who was lord of the manor, and Nicholas Ashton of Woolton Hall. In the nineteenth century many large houses were built in the area by successful Liverpool merchants, including The Grange, at Gateacre and Allerton Tower. These houses all required large numbers of servants and economic growth in Woolton and Gateacre was stimulated by the need to provide accommodation for these servants, stabling for horses, and the area benefited from the extra trade generated locally.

In the early twentieth century Gateacre, also known as Little Woolton, was still a rural village surrounded by farmland. Today, although it still retains its village green in the centre, the farms have gone and much of the area was covered with housing in the 1950s. Woolton Local Board was established in 1866 and gradually set about improving facilities such as sewerage, drainage and street paving, and Woolton and Gateacre became part of the city of Liverpool in 1913. In 1969 both Woolton and Gateacre were designated as Conservation Areas in recognition of their unique character.

Woolton Old School, 1947.
A.H. Jones, A.H. Jones Collection 58.

Although this building, in School Lane, has a date stone of 1610, it is probably considerably earlier, as suggested by its gothic windows, and may well be the oldest building in the village. It has, unusually for a simple country school, been constructed of large blocks of sandstone, in some cases more than four feet long and weighing over five hundredweight. There are a number of early references to a school in the village and it could be one of the earliest elementary schools in the county. In the nineteenth century it fell into disuse and by the 1970s was used as a tool shed. By the 1980s it had been renovated and refurbished as a private residence and is now a nursery school.

Woolton Street was divided into two halves when the High Street and, later, Kings Drive, were constructed. This view shows the quieter, southern, portion. Before the construction of Speke Road, originally called Chapel Street, this was the main road south from the village and continued in a straight line past Woolton Hall towards Ashton Square, across what was then the village green. By the early 1700s, when Richard Molyneux built the north wing of Woolton Hall, the road had been diverted so that the traffic of the village did not pass immediately in front of the building. On the left the large building, with stone quoins, is the offices of the former Woolton Local Board, responsible for local administration. It was not until 1913 that Woolton became part of the city of Liverpool. The houses on the left still stand, but those on the right were demolished in 1958 and modern flats, quite out of keeping with the area, were built. The newsagent's shop, at number 44, despite having the name 'Brown' outside, was run by Mrs. Doris Tewkesbury in 1946.

Alfred H Jones.

The Cross, Woolton village, 1946.
A.H. Jones, A.H. Jones Collection 32.

Woolton's village cross stands in Woolton Street, close to its junction with Speke Road, and may date back as far as the fourteenth century. Then the village was just a small group of farm cottages, only a few of which would have been built of the local sandstone. In 1913, to celebrate Woolton's incorporation into Liverpool, the top of the cross was restored by Arthur Stanley Mather, Lord Mayor of Liverpool in 1915/16 and resident of Woolton. The house in the background, with the elegant classical porch, is Engleberg, occupied in 1946 by a Mrs. Baker, with Brown's newsagent to the left.

108

Woolton Street, 1946.
A.H. Jones, A.H. Jones Collection 44.

These cottages at numbers 21A and 23 Woolton Street, to the north of the High Street, were demolished when the modern Post Office was built. In 1946 Mrs Alice Gainey, confectioner, occupied number 23, to the right, and Mrs Viola Bailey, simply described as a shopkeeper, was at number 21A. Just out of view to the left is the Coffee House public house, and to the right are the Salisbury Farm buildings, now the Liverpool Cheese Company. These surviving buildings, together with those shown here, may well date back to the seventeenth century.

Woolton tram terminus, 1946.
A.H. Jones, A.H. Jones Collection 24.

In 1946 trams from the centre of Liverpool stopped at the central reservation in the High Street and the number 5 can be seen here. The extensive railed queuing area, to the right, suggest that considerable numbers of passengers were expected at busy times of the day, when everyone would have travelled to work in Liverpool on the tram. The buffers at the end of each track were designed to prevent trams running away down Kings Drive and were often used as seats. High Street, despite its ancient sounding name, was not constructed until after 1845 and the houses to the right were also built after this date. In the mid twentieth century the road was widened to form the dual carriageway shown here. The church spire in the distance belongs to St. James Methodist Church, on the corner of Church Road South, with its church hall on the opposite corner, seen here in front of the church. Liverpool's last tram ran in September 1957 and today this area is a small car park.

ALFRED·H·JONES.

Reynolds Park, although one of Liverpool's smaller parks, consisting of just 14 acres, is a hidden gem. James Reynolds was a Liverpool cotton broker, who also owned a Welsh castle and Levens Hall in Cumbria. The park was given to the people of Liverpool in 1929 to thank them for their contribution to the family's wealth through the city's trade. Sadly the mansion house, shown here in this view of 1948, was destroyed by fire in 1975 and has been replaced by a complex of sheltered housing, occupying the same site. Features of the park include a Yew Garden and outdoor dining area, designed by Leila Reynolds and Sir Charles Reilly in the late 1920s, and a walled garden, which would originally have supplied the house with vegetables and flowers. This, together with a ha-ha, had been built by the 1840s and now provides displays of summer bedding and herbaceous borders.

The Grange, Gateacre, 1948.
A.H. Jones, A.H. Jones Collection 90.

This spacious and opulent house, in Jacobethan style, was built in the second half of the nineteenth century by Sir Andrew Barclay Walker, the millionaire owner of Walker's Warrington brewery. A mid-twentieth century sale catalogue itemises the house's features, which included a drawing room, music room or library, dining room, morning room, billiard room, smoke room and twenty one bedrooms on two floors. There were also additional domestic offices with a butler's pantry and plate-safe, servants' hall, housekeeper's room, kitchen, scullery and larders. The grounds originally extended as far as Grange Lane, with a series of terraces descending the hillside. Sir Andrew Barclay Walker, twice mayor of Liverpool, is best known for his gift of the Walker Art Gallery to the city, but he also gave a library and reading room, as well as the village green to his local community of Gateacre.

Rose Brow, Gateacre, 1948.
A.H. Jones, A.H. Jones Collection 79.

In this view the chimneys of The Grange are just visible between the roofs of the buildings in the foreground, and to the right are the lodge and U-shaped stable block belonging to The Grange. The latter was built around a courtyard, with a partially glazed roof, and provided seven loose boxes, four stalls, a coach house, garage and living accommodation for four men. In the twentieth century The Grange became a hospital owned by the Order of the Sisters of Charity of St Vincent de Paul and then in 1970 a home for retired seamen run by the Apostleship of the Sea. By the first decade of the twenty-first century it has been converted into apartments. The sandstone house to the left of the stables has a 1787 datestone, but this appears to have been moved from its original position. It is named as Grange Cottage in the 1911 Liverpool Street Directory and by 1949 appears to be St. Anne's Nurses Home, possibly having a connection with the adjoining hospital.

This picture, taken from the same vantage point as the previous one, looks in the opposite direction, northwards along Woolton Road and Cuckoo Lane. The cottages at the junction are believed to be the first built in the village, in the early seventeenth century. At the extreme right

Corner of Rose Brow and Cuckoo Lane, 1948.
A.H. Jones, A.H. Jones Collection 86.

is a former smithy, designed by Cornelius Sherlock, which later became the Smithy Tuck Shop, a well known local landmark, with a

surprisingly large five bedroom house attached. Today the cottages have been demolished, presumably when the road was widened, and modern detached houses have been built in Cuckoo Lane; the old smithy shop became a cobbler's and is now a nursery.

114

Gateacre Brow, 1948.
A.H. Jones, A.H. Jones Collection 78.

These two cottages form part of a group of nineteenth century buildings on Gateacre Brow, in the centre of Gateacre village, close to the eighteenth century Unitarian Chapel and near the triangular village green. This pair, numbers 6 and 8, are typical of the village, built of local sandstone, with timber bay windows. In 1948, when this view was painted, Edward Dawson lived at number 6, but number 8 appears to have been unoccupied.

Although painted nearly forty years earlier than the previous view, this scene would have been just as recognisable to A. H. Jones working in the 1940s, as it is today. This striking building, by W. Aubrey Thomas, built in 1888-91 for the National Telephone Company as a local telephone exchange, has a sandstone lower floor and elaborate half-timbering above, with moulded panels in seventeenth century Flemish

Gateacre Brow, 1910.
F. Beattie, Beattie Collection 187.

style, depicting scenes from the Bible, and a curious corner turret. When Beattie painted this view the building had been taken over by the Post Office, but also housed a branch of Parr's Bank, with the premises of Thomas H. Mullock, saddler, next door. By the time Jones

visited in the 1940s there was a branch of the Prudential Assurance Company Ltd. there. Marsh Brothers, grocers and provision merchants, managed by Patrick Burke, had been replaced by the grocer's shop of W. Brooks and Co Ltd, and Miss Eveline Hitchen's greengrocers. Today the ground floor is used as office accommodation.

116

Gateacre's church is situated some distance from the centre of the village, beyond the former Cheshire Lines Railway, in what would have been open fields at the time of its construction. This imposing building, designed by Cornelius Sherlock was built between 1872 and 1874, in thirteenth century decorated Gothic style, of local red sandstone, like many other buildings in the area. Stained glass windows by William Morris and Co. were added in 1883. Originally built as a chapel of ease to Childwall parish church, it did not become independent until 1893. At the time that the picture was painted in 1948 the minister was the Rev Victor Davies.

This rural autumn scene shows the harvest gathered in and looks across the fields at Wambo Lane, towards Belle Vale Farm or Hall. From Beattie's title to the picture this farm was presumably once worked by someone called Harrison and was therefore known locally by this name, but by 1911 John Glover was the

Harrison's Farm, Belle Vale Road, Gateacre, 1911.
F. Beattie, Beattie Collection 192.

farmer. In the distance is the tower of what may be the stables attached to Belle Vale Hall. The sheaves of wheat have been stacked in stooks to dry, before being taken back to the farmyard,

where, at this date, they would probably have been threshed using a steam powered traction engine. Today this area has changed out of all recognition and is the site of Belle Vale Shopping Centre and Belle Vale Park

Lee Hall, Gateacre, 1948.
A.H. Jones, A.H. Jones Collection 94.

This fine house, built in 1773 by John Okill, a Liverpool shipbuilder and timber merchant, was described by Peter Fleetwood-Hesketh in 1955 as 'one of the most perfect of smaller Georgian houses in Lancashire'. Over the years it saw a number of different tenants, including Councillor John Hays Wilson, who opened the gardens and parkland to the public in the early 1880s. In the same period Tarbock Races, organised by the Croxteth Hunt Club, were run there. In 1869 the grounds were the venue for a huge Orange Day celebration which attracted a reported 100,000 people. When Jones painted this view in 1948 the house was already suffering from neglect, having been left sadly empty for nearly 60 years, with bushes encroaching on the ground floor. At one point it was used by local farmers as a potato store, the columns from the front façade were removed and sold, and by 1956 it was decided that the building was too dilapidated to be worth restoring and it was demolished. Lee Park Golf Club and the Lee Park estate, built in the 1970s and bounded by Caldway Drive, now occupy the land.

Belle Vale Pumping Station, 1948.
A.H. Jones, A.H. Jones Collection 81.

This impressive building, described by Jones as the Belle Vale Pumping Station, also known as the Netherley Water Works, was situated at Netherley Bridge, close to the junction of today's Netherley Road and Caldway Drive. In July 1875 Widnes Gas and Water Committee bought a field containing a borehole from Thomas and William Dutton for £2,360 18s 6d to supplement their town's water supply. This was one of a number of water works in the area serving Gateacre, Woolton and Huyton with Roby.

SPEKE AND OGLET

The only Speke in England is found here on the banks of the River Mersey, seven miles from the centre of Liverpool. In the early years of the twentieth century it was still a small village, surrounded by agricultural land, with the parish church of All Saints, built in 1876, at its heart. Today, however, the landscape has changed completely. Land was first acquired for an industrial estate in the 1930s, as the Corporation attempted to attract new manufacturers to the city to alleviate unemployment, and by the 1950s trades established included motor engineering, rubber, paint and furniture manufacturing. It was initially envisaged that 10,000 houses would be built, together with a 'super hospital', a golf course, an open-air swimming pool, a stadium, public halls, churches, schools and cemeteries. In 1921 the population of Speke was 3,666 and by 1955 this had risen to about 21,000, although the originally projected population of 55,000 was never achieved due to the interruption of building work during World War II. The creator of this 'model town for the whole country' was Sir Lancelot Keay, City Architect and Director of Housing for Liverpool from 1925 to 1948. However as manufacturing jobs were lost it sadly became one of the most deprived wards in the country, a far cry from Keay's original plans, although new retail parks and a much expanded airport are attempting to revive the area.

One feature which has survived all these changes is Speke Hall, a Grade 1 listed building and one of the finest examples of a timber-framed building in the country. The house was built by the Norris family, reaching its present form in 1598, as recorded by Edward Norris over the main entrance. As part of his plan for the development of Speke Keay ensured that the small hamlet of Oglet, on the banks of the Mersey, south of Speke, and the eastern portion of the township, towards Hale, were protected as greenbelt land, which has preserved a small part of the original character of the area. Oglet now has a forlorn air and is probably more isolated than it has ever been, separated from Speke by the vast expanse of the runway of Liverpool John Lennon Airport.

Speke Church Road, Speke, 1950.
A.H. Jones, A.H. Jones Collection 144.

In 1901 Speke's population was just 381 and, although just seven miles from the centre of Liverpool, it must at this time have seemed very distant. Building work on the new estate started in 1937 and by the end of World War II 900 houses had been built, some of which are visible in the distance in this picture. However in the foreground are some houses from the original village of Speke, looking along Speke Church Road, towards the junction with Speke Town Lane, to the left, Blackrod Avenue (formerly Smithy Lane) on the right and Woodend Lane straight on. The familiar figure of a woman wheeling a pram, seen in other views, is also present here.

ALFRED·H·JONES·

Speke Town Lane, 1950.
A.H. Jones, A.H. Jones Collection 145.

At one time Speke Town Lane connected directly with Speke Hall Avenue, via Speke Town, a small hamlet of houses and a farm, half a mile north west of the church. These houses in Speke Town Lane, numbers 62, 63 and, by some strange numbering system, 13, were occupied at this date by Thomas McNally, labourer, John Ball, also a labourer, and iron worker Robert Edward Squires. Shortly after this picture was painted the buildings were demolished and the shops of The Crescent built on the site.

ALFRED H JONES

The long, low building seen here is the old smithy, which stood at the junction of Smithy Lane (later Blackrod Avenue) and Woodend Lane. A local directory published in 1889 reveals that the local smith was John Barrow. The new houses of Speke Church Road and

Smithy Lane, Speke, 1950.
A.H. Jones, A.H. Jones Collection 147.

Greyhound Farm Road can be seen here and the ground to the right, where the houses shown in the two previous views stood, has been cleared

to make way for the construction of The Crescent. The smithy was obviously empty and boarded up when the picture was painted but it later became Speke's first public library, finally closing in 1967 and demolished in 1969 when the structure became unsafe.

Speke Hall, 1858.
William Herdman, Herdman Collection 324.

Speke Hall survives as an oasis of calm amid the roar of jets at Liverpool John Lennon Airport to the east, and industrial and retail parks to the north and west. It is approached along a tree lined avenue and still appears much as it did in this view, looking from the south east and painted by William Herdman in 1858. The house is one of four outstanding surviving timber-framed buildings in the north of England and was built by the Norris family, primarily William Norris II and his son Edward, in stages, during the sixteenth century. However there are records of a John and Nichola de Norreys living here as early as 1314 and the remnants of a cruck frame have been found in the south east corner. By the end of the eighteenth century the house had passed into the hands of the Beauclerk family and fallen into disrepair. When purchased, for the only time in its history, by Liverpool merchant Richard Watt in 1795, it was derelict and contained no furniture.

Speke Hall, 1955.
Allan P. Tankard, Binns Collection C301.

Full restoration work on Speke Hall was not carried out until the middle of the nineteenth century by Richard Watt V, a descendent of the original Richard. Sadly Richard Watt V died young in 1865 and the estate passed to his eight year old daughter Adelaide, who became the final owner of Speke Hall. Later, influences of the Arts and Crafts movement were added by the Liverpool ship owner Frederick Leyland, who rented Speke Hall in the 1860s and 1870s, before Adelaide reached her majority. This view shows the west side of the house, viewed from the gardens, with the billiard room at the left hand corner. This had originally been used as a kitchen and was described as a complete wreck before Frederick Leyland carried out restoration work on the building in the 1870s, which included reglazing the windows, as well as the installation of a new stone floor and fireplace.

Speke Hall, 1955.
Allan P. Tankard, Binns Collection C295.

Adelaide Watt never married and she spent her life preserving and enhancing Speke Hall and its estate. After her death in 1921 the estate was sold to Liverpool Corporation and the land used for its new airport, industrial estate and housing. In 1943 the house was acquired by the National Trust, which continues to manage the building and gardens. This view shows the north entrance, with a bridge across the former moat, leading through a vestibule to the central courtyard. Until the restoration work in the nineteenth century the main entrance was on the far side of this courtyard.

Built about 1616 of local sandstone, this cottage stood at the far end of Oglet Lane, close to where the extension to Dungeon Lane now connects the two. Oglet Lane once ran from Hale Road south and then eastwards, parallel with the River Mersey, but has been cut in two by the construction of the new runway at Liverpool

Oglet Lane, Speke, 1949.
A.H. Jones, A.H. Jones Collection 119.

John Lennon Airport in 1966. Speke Airport, which opened in 1933, was situated further to the west and the original buildings continued in use until 1986. In the mid twentieth century this cottage was occupied by Thomas Hulme, his wife and their eleven children, although lack of space in such a small building meant that two of the children had to sleep at their grandmother's. The building was not demolished until the 1970s.

Oglet Lane, Speke, 1949.
A.H. Jones, A.H. Jones Collection 120.

These thatched cottages, numbers 59 and 61 Oglet Lane, are described by the artist as fishermen's cottages, and in the past, before the River Mersey became polluted by industrial waste, they were occupied by fishermen. The river was an excellent source of fresh fish, salmon, spelt and sparling upstream, and flat fish downstream. In addition the hamlet was well known for its shrimps, like Parkgate on the Wirral and Marshside, near Southport. The fish would have found a ready market in the growing town of Liverpool and Oglet women were a familiar site in Garston, where they walked to sell their baskets of shrimps. In 1901 the cottages were occupied by George Dubavin, his wife and daughter at number 59, and Henry Dunbavin, age 82, his son Thomas, age 56, and his grandson Henry, age 27, at number 61. All the men are described as fishermen and this surname is found a number of times in the Speke area. By 1949 Mrs Mary Elizabeth Camm and John Lea were living in the cottages.

This cottage, also in Oglet Lane, was originally two dwellings, and with the door to the right-hand property crudely bricked up, the entire building seems to be in a somewhat dilapidated state. The old fashioned hay wain on the right

Oglet Lane, 1949.
A.H. Jones, A.H. Jones Collection 121.

has had a roof added to give some protection to its cargo. A rental of 1460 for Oglet specified that each tenant, with land over a particular value, had to fetch two cartfuls of hay from the meadow as part of their service to lord of the manor. Those who tenanted land of lesser value had to assist with the haymaking or pay one (old) penny.

Oglet Lane, 1949.
A.H. Jones, A.H. Jones Collection 122.

This is Oglet Farm, situated close to the bend in Oglet Lane where it turns eastwards. Today it is no longer a working farm, but it is still a private house and the outbuildings have been converted into two homes. As well as bringing in the hay harvest, fifteenth century tenants had to dig turf, which would have been the most readily available fuel at this time, or pay a penalty of two pence to the lord of the manor. In the late nineteenth century this was one of the best wheat growing areas in south west Lancashire, with barley and oats also grown on the light sandy or stiff clay soils. In 1901 Thomas Tushingham lived here with his wife, Mary, and their seven children, the entire family having been born in Speke.

Known as Yew Tree Farm, this was probably the most substantial house in the small hamlet of Oglet and still stands today, although apparently empty. The 1901 census indicates that the farm was occupied by Henry Hatch, a gas works manager and, somewhat unusually, it is his wife, Annie, who describes herself as a farmer and employer. Farmer Aaron Harrison Cartwright lived there in 1949 when the picture was painted. The area around Oglet was not just devoted to agriculture; there were salt works on the shore and a ship breaker's yard at the bottom of Dungeon Lane. The cabins from the ships broken up here were sometimes used as sheds by the locals, or even as temporary housing for seasonal Irish farm workers. This is confirmed by the 1901 census which lists a number of farms in the Speke area having a 'shanty' on their land, all occupied by single young Irish agricultural labourers.

OUTSIDE THE CITY:
HALE AND HUYTON

Hale is situated on the banks of the River Mersey 9½ miles south east of Liverpool, but, despite the proximity of Liverpool airport it still retains a village atmosphere, with its church, manor house (formerly the parsonage) and cottages dating from the seventeenth to nineteenth centuries. From at least the twelfth century there was an important ford across the Mersey at Hale, to Weston on the south bank, which would have saved many miles of travel on poor roads, and which continued in use until the middle of the nineteenth century. However this route, especially in mist, was treacherous and in the churchyard there are a number of graves of those who drowned whilst trying to make the crossing. Hale was given its charter in 1203, four years before Liverpool, and the village also had a mayor, now termed a Lord Mayor, from a similar date.

Huyton was once a village of farms, cottages and large mansions, but after World War II it became one of the fastest growing districts of Liverpool, when large numbers of people were moved out of the city as a result of slum clearance programmes. Unlike Liverpool it was mentioned in the Domesday Book and its church, St. Michael's, which has its origins in the medieval period, was built on an ancient religious site. Sadly much of the old village was demolished in 1945 when the new town centre was built.

Manor House, Hale, 1945.
A.H. Jones, A.H. Jones Collection 101.

The elegant eighteenth century façade of the Manor House at Hale hides a building which is not all that it seems. It was once the parsonage and the original building was constructed in the seventeenth century, a fact which becomes apparent from the rear, where a two-storied structure, with two gables, is revealed. The classical sandstone façade, shown here, was added in the early eighteenth century, when Rev. William Langford was the local vicar and his arms are included in the scrolled pediment over the main door. The ambitious scheme to remodel and 'gentrify' the house appears never to have been completed as once it turns the corner the pediment on the right-hand side finishes abruptly. Later becoming a farmhouse, known as Manor Farm, it was occupied by the military for a time during World War II.

St Mary's Church, Church Road, Hale, 1949.
A.H. Jones, A.H. Jones Collection 107.

A chapel has stood on this site since at least the eleventh century and the parish registers start in 1590. However over the years there have been a number of rebuildings, including replacing a fourteenth century building in 1758-9, and further restoration work in 1874 and 1903. In 1977 a disastrous fire, set by vandals, left the old church gutted with only the walls and the fourteenth century tower standing. The parish registers, still kept in the church at that time, were also badly damaged. However the church has now been restored, with a newly designed interior, and from the outside it looks much as it did when this picture was painted in 1949. In the churchyard is the grave of John Middleton, better known as the Childe of Hale, born there in 1578, who grew to the height of 9 feet 3 inches. He was the bodyguard of Sir Gilbert Ireland, who had connections with the area, and became a national celebrity when he beat the champion of King James I in a wrestling match. His cottage still stands in the village, with the ceiling specially raised to allow for his height and the hat pegs fixed ten feet from the floor.

Police Station, Town Lane, Hale, 1949.
A.H. Jones, A.H. Jones Collection 110.

Hale Police Station still stands at number 44 Town Lane and is a typical rural police station, with living accommodation attached. It is interesting to note that Hale was considered large enough to have its own police station at this date. In 1901 the local constable was Abraham Clark, who lived at the station with his wife Mary, his sons Herbert, Walter and Hubert, and his daughters Edith and Ethel. Today the police station has closed and the buildings are private residences.

Hall Lane, Huyton, 1949.
A.H. Jones, A.H. Jones Collection 165.

This basically unremarkable scene typifies the way in which the artist has recorded everyday life, with the mother pushing a young child in a rather old-fashioned push chair. Hall Lane, running parallel to the Liverpool to Manchester Railway line, connects St John's Road and Wood Lane, where it crosses the railway line. On the corner of Seel Street, opposite, are the premises of John Cooper, greengrocer and beyond the junction is the Seel Arms public house, named after the adjacent Seel Road, with the licensee in 1949, John Michael Robinson.

Ivy Cottages, Huyton Lane, 1952.
A.H. Jones, A.H. Jones Collection 171.

This group of three cottages stood at right-angles to Huyton Lane close to St. Michael's Church, which can be seen in the background of this picture. In 1949 they were occupied by Clarence Edmund Jackson, an electrical contractor, Richard Goodson, a butcher and William M Simpson, a manager. St. Michael's

Church, Huyton is one of the area's few medieval churches, although there was probably a religious building on the same site even before. Built of local red sandstone, it has

weathered badly and has been much altered over the centuries. The chancel screen dates from about 1500, but was removed 'in time of rebellion', in 1647, and replaced again in 1663. The hammerbeam roof dates from a similar period. The church has two fonts, one Norman and the other in Perpendicular style.

This view looks along Huyton Lane, from its junction with Blue Bell Lane and Derby Lane, in the opposite direction to the previous picture, with the church out of sight on the left. On the right-hand side are the offices of Home James Coaches, which operated coach tours in the Liverpool area for many years. They also had premises in Wavertree, Sefton Park and Scotland Road. The Lancashire County Fire Brigade had its Station no.3 in Huyton Lane and the demolition work in progress just beyond the first house may be in connection with this.

INDEX

FURTHER READING

Barker, Eddie, *In and around Broad Green*, The Author, 1991.

Belchem, John (ed), *Liverpool 800; culture, character and history*, Liverpool University Press, 2006.

Cooper, John and David Power, *A history of West Derby*, Causeway Books, 1982, repr. 1987.

Griffiths, Robert, *The history of the royal and ancient park of Toxteth*, Liverpool Libraries and Information Services, 1907 repr, 2001.

Hoult, James, *West Derby, Old Swan and Wavertree*, Liverpool Libraries and Information Services, 1913 repr. 2005.

Liverpool Heritage Bureau, *Buildings of Liverpool*, Liverpool City Planning Department, 1978.

Moscardini, Anthony, *Woolton and Gateacre: architecture and heritage*, The Bluecoat Press, 2008.

Old Ordnance Survey maps, reprints of 25 inch to 1 mile maps of Liverpool, with historical notes, published by Alan Godfrey, 1989-2002.

Parrott, Kay, *West Derby and Norris Green*, Chalford, 1996.

Picton, J.A., *Memorials of Liverpool, historical and topographical*, 2 vols., Longmans, Green and Co., 1875.

Pollard, Richard and Nicholas Pevsner, *Lancashire: Liverpool and the south-west*, Yale University Press, 2006.

Whale, Derek, *The lost villages of Liverpool*, 3 vols., T. Stephenson, 1985.